Sticky Situations

Sticky Situations

Case Studies for Early Childhood Program Management

Sarah Taylor Vanover

ROWMAN & LITTLEFIELD
Lanham • Boulder • New York • London

Published by Rowman & Littlefield
A wholly owned subsidiary of The Rowman & Littlefield Publishing Group, Inc.
4501 Forbes Boulevard, Suite 200, Lanham, Maryland 20706
www.rowman.com

Unit A, Whitacre Mews, 26-34 Stannary Street, London SE11 4AB

Copyright © 2017 by Sarah Taylor Vanover

All rights reserved. No part of this book may be reproduced in any form or by any electronic or mechanical means, including information storage and retrieval systems, without written permission from the publisher, except by a reviewer who may quote passages in a review.

British Library Cataloguing in Publication Information Available

Library of Congress Cataloging-in-Publication Data Available
Names: Vanover, Sarah.
Title: Sticky situations : case studies for early childhood program management / Sarah Vanover.
Description: Lanham : Rowman & Littlefield, [2017]
Identifiers: LCCN 2016044333 | ISBN 9781475830835 (cloth : alk. paper) | ISBN 9781475830842 (pbk. : alk. paper)
Subjects: LCSH: Early childhood education—United States—Administration. | Early childhood education—United States—Case studies.
Classification: LCC LB2822.6 .V36 2017 | DDC 372.21—dc23
LC record available at https://lccn.loc.gov/2016044333

©™ The paper used in this publication meets the minimum requirements of American National Standard for Information Sciences—Permanence of Paper for Printed Library Materials, ANSI/NISO Z39.48-1992.

Printed in the United States of America

*This book is dedicated to Beth Morton,
who has been a fabulous early childhood program director
for both of my sons!
Thank you for doing a hard job and doing it well!*

Contents

Preface ix

1 A Sticky Situation with Marketing and Enrollment 1
2 A Sticky Situation with Menu Planning 5
3 A Sticky Situation with Parent Complaints 9
4 A Sticky Situation with Dress Code 13
5 A Sticky Situation with Cell Phones 17
6 A Sticky Situation with Biting 23
7 A Sticky Situation with Confidentiality 29
8 A Sticky Situation with Parent Feedback 35
9 A Sticky Situation with Staff Gossip 39
10 A Sticky Situation with Social Media 43
11 A Sticky Situation with Staff Playground Behavior 47
12 A Sticky Situation with Parent Behavior 53
13 A Sticky Situation with Annual Evaluations 59
14 A Sticky Situation with an Advisory Board 63
15 A Sticky Situation with Facility Management 67

16	A Sticky Situation with Weather Cancellations	71
17	A Sticky Situation with Staff Interviews	75
18	A Sticky Situation with Parent Education Nights	81
19	A Sticky Situation with Fund-Raising	85
20	A Sticky Situation with Staff Turnover	91
21	A Sticky Situation with Staff Professional Development	95
22	A Sticky Situation with Scheduling	99
23	A Sticky Situation with Transportation	105
24	A Sticky Situation with Staff Wages	109
About the Author		113

Preface

I first became the director of an early childhood education program after I spent eight years as an assistant and lead teacher. At that point, I had a great awareness of child development principles, a solid understanding of early childhood curriculum, and a working knowledge of children with special needs. I found out quickly that those skills were only one tool in the entire tool kit for being a successful program manager.

Quite frequently, the tasks that took the largest portions of my time were tasks with which I had no formal training. Even though someone else was responsible for our center payroll, I was still charged with establishing and managing the center budget. Although I could hire contractors to come to the center for facility repairs, I needed to know enough about facility management to determine a schedule for routine maintenance and to evaluate reasonable costs for unscheduled repairs. I had no training in marketing, but I needed to find a way to advertise our program for potential clients and potential employees. I had limited experience with grant writing and fund-raising, but I needed to find additional sources of income to take some of the burden off tuition costs.

My daily tasks as a director included scheduling, staffing, building relationships with parents and staff members, and improving the level of professionalism throughout the center. I was not trained on supervising staff or evaluating staff performance when I completed my degree in early childhood education. These were the skills that I learned while I was on the job, and honestly, I learned by trial and error.

When I first put together a parent handbook and an employee handbook for my center, I had a basic idea of policies that the center needed, but those handbooks evolved over time as I encountered more and more unusual situations and needed to create a way for the teaching staff to handle those interesting situations. After hiring several employees who were not a good match for the needs of my center, I changed the ways that I conducted interviews. A great deal of my knowledge came from facing a new experience and having to sit down and think through the best way to handle that situation for the children, families, and staff members involved.

Sticky Situations: Case Studies for Early Childhood Program Management is a collection of case studies that will allow early childhood educators to review possible situations that they may encounter as a program director and resolve the situations in the best possible way. Many of these case studies do not have one correct answer. There are reminders and discussion questions with each case study to help the early childhood specialist remember best practice and to evaluate the performance of the program manager in each case study. It is my hope that this text better prepares future early childhood managers for the difficult situations they will encounter in their careers.

Chapter 1

A Sticky Situation with Marketing and Enrollment

Alicia is the director of a small childcare program that can serve seventy-five children from infants through preschoolers when fully enrolled. The program has a long-standing, positive reputation in the community, and simple word-of-mouth has kept her program at full capacity for many years. In the past three years, enrollment has begun to dwindle because two other childcare programs have opened in the same neighborhood.

Although Alicia's center has lost only about eight spots, it has caused her to let two staff members go. She has been reviewing the center's income over the past few months, and it looks like she will need to let one more staff member go if she cannot increase enrollment. Since Alicia's program is not taking in as much tuition, she doesn't have the income to pay as many employees.

Her center has a lot of benefits that she can promote in the community. The program has low student-to-teacher ratios, educated teaching staff, and a kindergarten readiness curriculum for the students. Once families come to see the center and tour the classrooms, they are almost always interested in filling out an application, but recently, fewer families are setting up a tour of the program.

Right now, Alicia has to figure out the best way to get families into the center to view the program firsthand. Some of the methods that she has used to advertise in the past don't seem as effective as they used to be. Newspaper advertising is now extremely expensive, and many community members do not read the newspaper anymore.

Alicia recently invested in redesigning the center's website and creating a social media page for program activities, but those are utilized primarily by families who already know information about the center. One parent told her that he initially learned about the program from a family friend's T-shirt with the school logo on the front. Once he saw the shirt, he asked the family about the school, and the family gave him rave reviews.

Alicia has a limited budget for marketing. Approximately 75 percent of the center budget goes toward staff salaries, and the rest of the budget must cover facilities, meals for the children, curriculum supplies, and marketing costs. In an attempt to be as effective as possible with her marketing budget, she decides to talk to her currently enrolled families to determine how they first learned about her childcare program. The overwhelming response from her enrolled families is that a friend of the family or a currently enrolled family gave them a personal recommendation that the center offers a high-quality program. After the recommendation, the prospective family contacted the center for a tour.

She knows that several other childcare programs in town have used community events like maternity fairs, preschool fairs, and arts and craft fairs to distribute information about their childcare centers. There is usually a cost to set up a booth at these events, and she would also need to pay staff to attend these events on evenings or weekends. Even though other centers have used these community events to distribute information, Alicia does not know if these events were successful at recruiting new families.

There are other community organizations like pediatricians' offices, online discussion boards, and public libraries that may be willing to distribute information about her childcare program, but many of these organizations require that she receive special approval from the administrator in order to distribute information.

Alicia needs to make a plan to educate the community about her childcare program and to increase enrollment. What should she do next?

REMINDERS

- Currently enrolled families are the greatest resource. Use them!
- It is important to ask for help if areas like marketing make early childhood educators uncomfortable. Consider what resources are

available. A parent or board member may have experience with marketing or advertising. Make sure to ask for their guidance.
- Free media or advertising may be available in the community. It is important to look for opportunities like local news programs or community fairs.
- In many cases, the community may never have heard about the childcare program. A directors need to find ways to get the name of his or her center out into the city. Simple ideas like t-shirts with the center logo may help raise community awareness.

ACTION PLAN

In order to best use her resources, Alicia decides to offer a $100 tuition credit to any currently enrolled families that refer a family to her childcare program and that family enrolls and begins in the childcare program. She also decides that more families need to know about the program. If they could see the program, she thinks that they would want to enroll. She reaches out to the children's event coordinator for the city's philharmonic orchestra, and she offers her facility for free as the site for one of their upcoming children's community programs. This will allow community families to tour her center and see what the program has to offer.

She also contacts one of the local parent support groups in town and offers for them to use her site as the location for their annual preschool fair if she can display a table for her center free of charge. This will allow her to distribute materials to families at no cost and get more families from the community to get a free tour of the facility.

DISCUSSION QUESTIONS

- Does Alicia's plan effectively use her resources? If not, what would be a better way to use her marketing budget?
- What is the best way to advertise the referral program to her currently enrolled families?
- If she still needs additional advertising, what should be her next step?

Chapter 2

A Sticky Situation with Menu Planning

Ben's childcare program has had the same menu for the past three years, and the parent advisory board for his center has asked Ben to make some revisions to the menu. His center provides a hot breakfast, a hot lunch, and an afternoon snack each day to the children enrolled, and currently he has a three-week menu rotation.

Ben serves breakfast and lunch to eighty-four children and an afternoon snack to approximately one hundred children, including those who are there for his school-age afterschool program. When additional food is prepared, Ben offers that food to his staff, but he does not guarantee the staff that he can feed them each day.

His program participates in the federal food program, so the menu must meet those guidelines for serving size and for the food groups represented for each meal and snack. He also wants to make sure that the menu allows children to eat independently without assistance from adults.

The parents first approached Ben about possibly revising the menu at the October board meeting. One group of parents began the conversation about the menu by saying that they would like to see healthier food options on the weekly menu. They have requested more organic food options, and they have asked that all fried foods be removed from the center's menu.

Ben is certain that he can make some healthier changes to the menu. He can switch to whole wheat bread. He can make sure that he switches any fried items to baked instead. Ben can change the milk from 2 percent milk to skim milk for children who are over two years old. Any more significant changes will require him to contact his food vendor to look more closely at the pricing guide.

Another group of parents also spoke out at the meeting with concerns about their children coming home hungry each day. They want to make sure that the menu has some childhood favorites like chicken nuggets and spaghetti. The lunch menu has a protein, a fruit, a vegetable, a grain, and a dairy product served each day. Even with a variety of fruits and vegetables served, the most popular menu items in the center continue to be chicken nuggets, pizza, macaroni and cheese, fish sticks, and fresh fruit.

Even though Ben is willing to make changes to the menu, he still needs to consider many factors. First, incorporating more organic foods will significantly increase the cost of the menu. Since the majority of the school budget is devoted to paying staff salaries, there is not available funding to increase the food budget significantly. Also, if the menu is altered to include healthier selections, will the children still eat the items that he is serving? There are already parents who have concerns about their children coming home hungry.

Ben was previously a director at a smaller childcare program, and the same discussion came up at that center. He made an attempt to make the menu healthier, but then the staff noticed that they were throwing away a great deal of the food each day. This meant that not only were children going home hungry, but he was also wasting money on food that was not eaten.

Ben has asked parents and classroom teaching staff to suggest sample meals that they believe the children will eat. As he reviews the sample menus, he compares them to several specialized menu requests that he needs to keep in mind. He has two children in the center who are severely allergic to peanuts, so Ben decides to have a peanut-free menu. He also has two children who are allergic to strawberries, three children who are allergic to citrus fruit, and one child with celiac disease who needs a gluten-free diet.

In addition to the children having food allergies, Ben has two families in his center who do not eat pork due to religious beliefs, and there is one vegetarian family. Due to a large list of accommodations, he needs to decide if he will provide an alternate menu for each child, or if he will provide one menu each day and allow families to bring their own breakfast, lunch, or snack if the food provided does not meet the needs of the children.

A Sticky Situation with Menu Planning

If families do bring an alternate menu, then Ben will need to find a way to ensure that families understand the requirements of the federal food program. If a child brings lunch from home, but the meal does not contain the required food items and portion sizes, then the childcare program will be responsible for supplementing that menu to meet the minimum requirements.

What type of changes will Ben need to make to the menu? Should he accommodate all the dietary needs of each child enrolled in the program? How will he ensure that he is providing a healthy menu, but the foods are still child-friendly?

REMINDERS

- Ben can view the federal food program requirements at http://www.fns.usda.gov/cacfp/child-and-adult-care-food-program.
- There may be additional food requirements provided from his state licensing agency, so he must make sure to review state laws on child care meal requirements.
- There is no set requirement on how long a menu rotation should be. Many childcare programs plan between three and five weeks of menus and rotate those weekly menus.
- Some childcare programs do not provide meals for participants, and all families must pack a lunch. These facilities do not participate in the federal food program, but they may still have state licensing laws that require them to ensure that children receive the required nutrition each day even if the child's family packs the meal.

ACTION PLAN

Ben decides to begin with some simple changes to the menu. Children who are two years old and older will receive skim milk with meals. He will also switch all breads and cereals to whole grain. It will be too costly to provide fresh fruits and vegetables every day, but he can try to include more on the menu instead of the canned or frozen alternative. Ben decides to begin by including two fresh fruits per week. He also decides to replace all fried foods with a baked alternative and include sweet potatoes and squash on the menu to integrate new vegetables.

Although Ben doesn't want to replace entrées that the children enjoy a great deal, he begins by asking the teachers about which meals seem to be the least popular. Ben finds out that Salisbury steak and Sloppy Joes are the least popular meals. He can substitute two of the sample meals suggested by parents into the current menu in place of these two entrées.

Due to the size of the center, it is not possible to individualize each meal. Ben does decide to offer a peanut-free menu due to the risk of anaphylaxis. He decides that all other menu modifications must be provided by the family. He is still required to make sure that each child meets the food requirements provided by the federal food program.

Ben creates a handout for the families to explain what nutritional requirements must be included in breakfast, lunch, and the afternoon snack. He also includes the information about the required portion size and a statement that explains that if these requirements are not met, then the school will supplement the child's meal.

DISCUSSION QUESTIONS

- Do you believe that Ben's changes to the menu will meet the requests of the parents?
- How should Ben communicate these changes to the families?
- If parents ask why he has not made more changes, what should Ben tell them? If they ask for more individualized menus due to allergies or religious beliefs, what information should Ben share with them?

Chapter 3

A Sticky Situation with Parent Complaints

Rachel, the director of the Brighton Center for Children, has invested a great deal of time in developing relationships with the parents at her childcare program. She makes an effort to be in the main hallway each morning during drop-off time to greet all the parents. She knows each parent's first name and what his or her job is, and she always speaks to as many parents as possible at school-wide events. Most of the parents in her program feel very comfortable coming to Rachel when they have a concern about the center or their child's classroom.

Ms. Jackson came to Rachel's office a couple of months ago to talk about the paint easel in her son's classroom. Ms. Jackson told Rachel that two of her son's T-shirts have been ruined because the paint that the classroom teachers are providing will not come out of his T-shirts. Rachel suggested that Ms. Jackson's son not wear his nicest clothes to school so that he can play without having to worry about stains or getting dirty. Ms. Jackson told Rachel that all of her son's clothes are nice, and she will have to purchase new clothing that he can get dirty. Rachel told Ms. Jackson that she appreciated her expressing her concerns with her directly.

A few days later, Ms. Jackson came to speak with Rachel again. Her son was on the playground when she arrived to pick him up from school. The temperature was in the low 90s, and Ms. Jackson felt that it was too hot for a young child to be outside playing. Rachel explained to Ms. Jackson that the center follows all weather advisories for extreme temperatures, but if there are no advisories in place, then the children go outside to play twice a day for thirty minutes each.

When the families bring in sunscreen and sign a permission slip for the sunscreen to be applied, then each child has sunscreen on when he or she goes outside in warm weather. The teachers also take water outside for the children to drink when they are playing so that no one becomes dehydrated. During the hottest summer months, the teachers also plan "water play days" when the children can play in the sprinklers. There is a shade structure on the playground so that children can cool off in the shade.

Ms. Jackson says that she would prefer her son to stay inside in the afternoon when the rest of the children go out to play. Rachel explains that there is not enough staff to keep one teacher inside with Ms. Jackson's son. She tells Ms. Jackson that she is welcome to send in additional sunscreen or his own water bottle.

The classroom goes outside every afternoon at the same time, so Ms. Jackson also has the option to pick her son up from school before the children go outside to play. Ms. Jackson says that she will consider her options, and she says goodbye to Rachel.

Rachel continues to say hello to Ms. Jackson each day in the hallway, but the next week Ms. Jackson visits Rachel's office again. This time she is upset because her son wore home a pair of pink shorts the day before. Rachel said that she did not know why he wore the pink shorts home, but she would go ask the teachers about them.

When Rachel asked the teachers about the pink shorts, they told her that the little boy had had an accident on the way to the restroom and he did not have any extra clothes from home. The teachers had to use the extra clothing they had stored in the classroom, and the only pair of shorts that fit him happened to be pink.

Rachel waited for Ms. Jackson to come and pick up her son that afternoon and shared this information with her, and she also encouraged Ms. Jackson always to speak with the teachers first about these types of questions since they are in the classroom with her son each day.

The following day, Ms. Jackson returned to Rachel's office, but this time, she was not alone. Ms. Jackson and Ms. Bryant both came to see Rachel. They were concerned that the teacher gave the children ice pops on the playground the previous day afternoon. Ms. Jackson said that she does not let her son have treats with artificial colors and sweeteners, so she was upset that the teacher gave her son the popsicle without her permission.

Rachel explained that the teacher offered the children the popsicles because it was a hot day outside, but if Ms. Jackson does not want her son to have a popsicle while in childcare, then the teacher can let her know in advance next time so that Ms. Jackson can provide an alternative treat for her son. Ms. Bryant said that she wanted the teacher to notify her as well, and Rachel said that she would speak to the teacher about both boys having an alternative treat for special occasions.

Rachel feels there is a great deal of stress between herself and Ms. Jackson. She must figure out a way to improve the relationship between them and help Ms. Jackson feel comfortable with her son at the Brighton Center for Children. What should she do?

REMINDERS

- Early childhood education programs are also small businesses, so it is essential to offer excellent customer service in order to build the best possible relationships with clients.
- Small businesses have limited resources, so they may not be able to meet the needs of every customer. When that is the case, customers have the option to keep their child in the current childcare center or look for a childcare center that best meets the needs of the family.
- Currently enrolled families can be the best marketing tool that a childcare program has. Other families frequently ask where their children are enrolled in childcare and if the family is happy with their current care. If a family is unhappy, they can discourage many other families from enrolling in the childcare program.
- When families are upset with a classroom teacher, the program administrator should always direct the family to speak with the teacher first and then seek the administrator's help if an agreement cannot be made.
- When a parent or guardian is overly involved in what is going on in the center, it may be beneficial for the program management to find a positive outlet for the parent to use his or her time and energy. This may be the perfect parent to organize a teacher appreciation lunch or help with a center-wide fund-raiser.

Chapter 3

ACTION PLAN

Several days after Ms. Jackson came to Rachel's office the last time, Rachel stopped her in the hallway during morning drop-off. She told Ms. Jackson that the Center for Children was looking for an additional fundraiser for the upcoming school year to raise money for new playground equipment. Rachel said that she knew Ms. Jackson toured many different preschools when selecting one for her son, so she was curious if Ms. Jackson knew how other programs were raising money for their centers.

Ms. Jackson told Rachel that she still had many of the parent handbooks and information at home and she would be happy to provide Rachel with a list of all the fundraiser information that she could find. Two days later Ms. Jackson brought Rachel a two-page list of local centers and their annual fundraiser efforts.

When Ms. Jackson was in Rachel's office, she mentioned that she noticed a small bruise on her son's arm the previous day evening, but there was no accident report provided by the teachers. Rachel suggested that Ms. Jackson speak with the classroom teachers to see if they remember her son bumping his arm yesterday afternoon.

Before Ms. Jackson left Rachel's office, Rachel asked her if she would be willing to look into what would be involved in the center sponsoring a one-day training event for other early childhood educators in the area. The center will need a parent committee to assist with the event if it decides to move forward. Since Ms. Jackson already knows so much about how well other centers are doing with their fundraiser efforts, Rachel thought that she would be a great asset to their planning committee. Ms. Jackson accepted and told Rachel that she would be happy to help with the planning.

DISCUSSION QUESTIONS

- Did Rachel give Ms. Jackson too much power in an attempt to make her feel more comfortable in the childcare program?
- Why is it essential for the administration to keep directing parents to speak with the classroom teachers before bringing concerns to the director?
- Is there ever a point when the director should admit to the family that they are at an impasse and must agree to disagree?

- The clothes and shoes that an employee wears to work should not limit his or her ability to care for the children, especially on the playground. A teacher should always be able to keep up with the pace of the children and even rush to their aid in the event of an emergency.
- A well-written policy can prevent the program director from having to make individual decisions about each employee's attire. It can prevent any discussion or reminders about dress code from being personal.

ACTION PLAN

Vaughn decides to begin by editing the current dress code to state that each employee must dress professionally when at work, and the policy further explains that he expects "business casual attire." He defines "business casual pants" as clean pants with pockets (including denim), but the policy does state that workout clothing, sweatpants, or pajama bottoms are *not* considered professional attire. He defines "business casual tops" as clean shirts with or without a collar that do not have large graphic designs on them (like athletic T-shirts). Employees may wear T-shirts with the school logo on them if they choose to purchase a shirt with their own money. The policy also states that "business casual attire" may not be low-cut and will show modesty.

The policy also states that hospital scrubs are not considered professional attire for educators, and they may not be worn to work. Teaching staff are expected to wear tennis shoes or footwear that allows them to run and climb on playground equipment with children. At the request of the advisory board, the policy states that tattoos and facial/body piercings may not be visible during the workday, so employees with tattoos or piercings must find a way to cover these items while at work.

Finally, Vaughn includes a section of the dress code that fashion accessories may be worn if they are not a risk to the staff members or the children for whom they are caring. For example, long earrings should not be worn because a child could easily pull on them, injuring the employee or possibly mouthing or ingesting the jewelry. A staff member must keep his or her fingernails at a shortened length to avoid scratching and hurting a small child.

Vaughn has no desire to remove denim jeans from the dress code because it would cost many of the employees a great deal of money to replace all of their jeans with other types of casual pants, and he believes that jeans look professional in an early childhood classroom as long as they do not have holes.

One of the board members suggested that Vaughn could resolve many of the dress code conflicts by requiring a standard uniform with polo shirts and tan pants for each staff member. Vaughn wanted to save this idea as a last resort if dress code issues continued because he wanted staff members to feel as comfortable as possible in their classrooms in their own clothing; however, it would be an option in the future if he needed it.

DISCUSSION QUESTIONS

- Do you believe that the changes that Vaughn intends to implement will improve the professional appearance of the staff members without causing too much resistance from the staff?
- Are these changes cost-effective for the staff members?
- What would be the benefits of a designated employee uniform?
- Is it appropriate to let early childhood professionals wear denim jeans as a part of their professional wardrobe?

Chapter 5

A Sticky Situation with Cell Phones

Although she has worked in the field of early education for several years, Annia has been the director of Small Beginnings Childcare only for two months. She is still learning about the staff members and the center operations. The employee handbook states that teachers may not use their cell phones during classroom time, but they may use them on their breaks. Some of the staff members follow this policy diligently, but Annia has noticed some teachers quickly hiding their cell phones when she walks into their classroom or when she is giving prospective parents tours of the building.

Since she is still so new to the program, Annia did not want to begin at her new center by singling out individuals and beginning a corrective action plan. After six weeks at her job, she decided to bring up the topic of cell phones at the bimonthly staff meeting. She reviewed the center policy that was written in the employee handbook, and she explained that this is an important policy that all the employees need to follow. She reiterated that if a staff member is using his or her cell phone in the classroom, then he or she is not devoting that time to watching the children and accidents could occur.

Several teachers at the staff meeting speak up and say that parents frequently text them during the day to check on their children, so they routinely check their phones to respond to parents as needed. Annia agrees that parent communication is an important component of their jobs, but the first priority for the teachers should be the children. It is their responsibility not only to keep them safe but also to play with them and have conversations during the school day. This is challenging when the teachers are constantly on their phones.

Annia encourages the teachers to tell parents they may always call the school and she or the assistant director can go down to the classrooms to check on the children. Redirecting the parents to make a phone call instead of a text may limit parents to only contacting the school with necessary information during the day.

Annia also reminds the teachers that using the school phone will allow staff members to have more privacy when they are away from school, since many of the staff members have parents who text them after hours and on weekends. In addition, Annia told the teachers that she would send out an email to the families about the preferred methods of contacting the classroom teachers during the school day.

After the staff meeting, Annia saw some improvement. More parents were calling the school to ask questions instead of texting the teacher directly. However, after a week, Annia began to notice more cell phones out in the classrooms again. Annia also noticed several teachers spending most of naptime on their cell phones instead of cleaning the classrooms or using the time to work on lesson plans.

At this point, Annia decided to speak to several teachers individually about using their cell phones in the classroom. One teacher told her that during naptime she was using the app for the school's assessment tool to upload assessment information about the children. Another teacher told her that she keeps her phone out to take pictures of the children for their portfolios and to send pictures to the parents.

Annia explained to the teacher that taking pictures of the children should not be a large focus during the school day. It is more important to spend time leading small group activities and talking with the children. She explained to the other teacher that she should not be completing assessment data on her app during classroom time. It is most important to give full attention to the children during classroom time and save paperwork for planning time.

Although teachers have been telling Annia that they are using their phones for work purposes, she begins to wonder if that is accurate. Even if they have the best intentions, it is so easy to check your email or text messages once your phone is within reach. Also, when parents come in to the center, they cannot tell if the teacher is using the phone for work or for personal use. They just see a teacher who is on the phone instead of interacting with their children.

The current policy explains that phones should not be in the classroom, but is the policy written efficiently? Does the policy need to be enforced differently?

Annia also has concerns about the college practicum students who come to the center to do volunteer hours for their education courses. The college students seem to be using their phones constantly when they are in the classroom. Annia contacts the supervising professor when this is a problem, but it does not prevent parents from seeing them use their phones in the classroom. Also, when Annia is giving tours to potential families, they do not know who is a staff member and who is a volunteer. If a potential family sees a volunteer continuously using his or her phone, will it deter them from selecting the program?

How should Annia proceed to make sure that teachers are focusing on the children in the classroom instead of using their cell phones?

REMINDERS

- There are many different ways that parents can communicate with teachers during the day. Communication does not have to hinge on cell phones.
- Some families may abuse the privilege of having a staff member's cell phone number and contact staff at inappropriate times. Every staff member should have a right to private time (outside of the work day) without being contacted by the families.
- Even a well-written policy is not effective if it is not enforced. Every director needs to think of what type of disciplinary actions should be taken if staff members do not follow center policy. The director must also make sure that the disciplinary action matches the severity of the staff behavior.
- If a director has an agreement with a local college or university to have their students in the childcare program classrooms, then there should be a written agreement of the behavior that is expected from the college students. If students cannot maintain that level of professionalism, then they may be asked to find an alternative volunteer placement. This agreement may include dress code, confidentiality, cell phone and social media use, and other professional behaviors.

Chapter 5

ACTION PLAN

Annia believes that the cell phone policy in the employee handbook is sufficient, except she wants to include one additional statement. She rewrites the policy to say:

- Employees should not use their cell phones in the classroom, but they may use them when on a break. If a classroom activity requires the use of the cell phone camera for a limited amount of time, the teacher must obtain permission from the center director.

Annia believes that the main problem with cell phone use in the building is that the policy has never been enforced before. She reviews the disciplinary action section of the employee handbook. It states that, in the event of a disciplinary action, the employee must first be given a verbal warning. If the employee continues the problem behavior after the verbal warning, then the administrator will offer a written warning with a corrective action plan that offers steps to resolve the problem. If the employee still continues the problem behavior after the written warning, then the administrator may terminate employment.

Although Annia has no desire to terminate employment of a staff member over cell phone use, she does believe that a couple of the staff members may need a written agreement stating that they will leave their cell phones in their cars during work hours. Each corrective action plan has an expiration date, so this type of agreement would only be a temporary solution until the problem behavior is resolved. Annia's greatest fear with continued cell phone use is that a child could get a more serious injury in the classroom due to a lack of supervision.

The student volunteers are also a concern for Annia. The written agreement between the college and Small Beginnings Childcare is very vague. Annia contacts the university faculty member who coordinates the student observers and asks her to meet to discuss their contract. Annia asks that the contract be changed to state that student observers must adhere to the employee handbook policies regarding confidentiality, dress code, cell phone use, social media accounts, and photography of children. She also outlines that all college students must have the same personnel paperwork (e.g., medical release forms and background checks) as all of the Small Beginnings staff. The university agrees to update the contract.

DISCUSSION QUESTIONS

- What are the best ways for a childcare director to enforce employee handbook policies?
- What type of negative outcomes or liabilities could the center face if the staff do not adhere to the cell phone policy?
- Did Annia's revision to the cell phone policy give the staff too much freedom?
- How can Annia and the university liaison make sure that student observers follow the contract requirements?

Chapter 6

A Sticky Situation with Biting

The toddler room at Kesha's childcare program has eight children between the ages of twelve and twenty-four months. Two teachers work in this classroom, and the center always maintains a ratio of one teacher to every four students. All of the toddlers in the classroom are mobile, but most of the children are not very verbal. The children can say familiar words like "cup" and "ball," but they are not yet able to communicate with each other very well.

Since children this age have a difficult time expressing themselves to each other, they often resort to hitting, scratching, or biting to get their points across when they are upset or frightened. The incident/accident forms that Kesha uses for the center have a spot for the director signature so that she can monitor how frequently these types of incidents occur.

In the past three weeks, Kesha has noticed that she has signed five incident reports for a little boy in the toddler room. Three of those reports were for biting. One report was for scratching a classmate, and the other report was for pushing a child, who bumped his head on the table during his fall.

Adam, the little boy who has been aggressive with his peers is eighteen months old, and he can say about two dozen words. When Kesha first recognizes this pattern, she goes to talk to the teacher about what they are doing in the classroom to prevent Adam from hurting his classmates.

The teachers have offered Adam some toys that he can chew on instead of biting. This includes a vibrating teething toy and some other chewy toys.

They have made it a priority to keep these clean for him so that he always has an option to chew on something instead of biting a friend.

The teachers have also been reading a children's book to Adam called *Teeth Are Not for Biting*. This book uses simple sentences to reinforce that children are not allowed to bite others. Finally, they have been working with all the children in the classroom to use the word "no" when another peer scares them or gets too close to them.

Kesha asks the toddler teachers to continue to enforce those strategies with the children, and she also sends home a handout for each family about toddlers and biting. The handout explains that it is a normal stage of development for a toddler to bite, and then it outlines methods to help a toddler who is struggling with biting others. At first, this seems to calm the parents' concerns, but as Adam continues to bite more of his classmates, parents begin complaining to the classroom teachers on a daily basis.

Kesha receives an email from a mother who is concerned that her daughter was bitten five times in the past month. Although the incident reports have all kept Adam's identity confidential, the mother knows that it is Adam who is biting her daughter. Kesha reassures the mother that this is a typical behavior in a toddler classroom, but she also offers to increase staffing in the room for the next week to reduce the problem and hopefully to help set new classroom behaviors.

For one week Kesha has three teachers in the toddler classroom with one teacher specifically shadowing Adam. During that time, Adam bites fewer children, but the biting continues, specifically at times when the teachers are needed elsewhere in the classroom. As soon as there are only two teachers in the classroom, the number of bites increases again.

At this point, three mothers of toddlers in the classroom all come to see Kesha at the same time. They know that Adam is the child who is biting other students, and the mothers would like to know what steps the school is taking to stop this behavior. Although the teachers and Adam's family have been meeting regularly to brainstorm how to resolve the situation, Kesha cannot give the mothers confidential information about Adam. Instead, she assures them that the school and the family are doing everything possible to resolve the problem.

When Kesha does not provide the three mothers with the information that they were seeking, Abigail's mother asks that Adam be removed from the classroom. She also states that she reviewed the family handbook, and there is no information listed about how the center handles a child who repeatedly bites or injures the other children in the classroom.

Kesha states that she will not expel a child for biting when it is a developmentally appropriate behavior. Abigail's mother then tells Kesha that she is giving her two weeks' notice for Abigail's withdrawal. Kesha says that the center will definitely miss having Abigail in the program, and then Abigail's mother leaves Kesha's office. One of the other mothers says that she has heard about childcare programs that expel children after a certain number of bites, and she wonders if Kesha couldn't implement a similar procedure.

Once Kesha is alone and has the opportunity to evaluate the situation in the toddler classroom, she decides it would be good for the center to have a standard procedure in place on how to deal with excessive biting.

REMINDERS

- Every toddler classroom is going to have biting because it is developmentally appropriate for that age.
- Every time a classroom has repeated biting occurrences, there will be parent complaints. It is the job of the parents to protect their children, so it is only natural for the family to voice their concerns when this happens, even if the parent is unreasonable. Some families may simply want you to hear their concerns, while others may demand an action.
- Biting can occur for many different reasons. A child may bite because he or she has limited language skills. A child may bite due to teething or sensory processing issues. Children may also bite to protect themselves if they feel threatened. It is essential to observe the child in the natural setting to see if you can determine a trigger and assess why the child is biting.
- It is very important to communicate with the family so that both the school and the parents are working to eliminate the negative behavior. This will create the best possible success story.

ACTION PLAN

Before writing any procedures, Kesha is determined that as long as the family of the child who is biting will work with the center to help resolve the issue, she will never expel a child from her program for biting. That is the end result that she must achieve. After looking back over the past few years, Kesha realizes that the center has been handling all biting episodes in this manner, even though a procedure has never been written down.

1. After a pattern of biting has developed in the classroom, the classroom teacher and director will sit down to discuss what changes to make in the classroom to eliminate this behavior.
2. The classroom teacher will make an appointment to speak with the family about how to implement these strategies at home, and the family and teacher will use similar techniques to maximize their success and eliminate confusion for the child.
3. The classroom teacher will provide information to the entire class about the developmental stage of biting and how to encourage your child to use other ways to express himself or herself.
4. If biting continues beyond these actions, then the family will be referred to the child's pediatrician for a developmental evaluation to see if speech pathology or occupational therapy may be needed to assist the child. The family will provide updates from the pediatrician or the therapist to help the center best serve the needs of the child.
5. The family will continue to meet regularly with the classroom teacher and director, as needed, until the behavior is resolved.
6. Families that partner with the center to improve the behavior problem will not be asked to leave the childcare program. If a family refuses to participate in this process, then they may need to seek other childcare arrangements.

Since Kesha is unable to share individual details with the classroom about how they are assisting Adam to stop him from biting, it may calm the parents to see the center procedure in print on what steps the center plans to take whenever there is a pattern of biting. The procedure can be added to the parent handbook as a reference for families who have any additional questions.

Since Adam has continued to bite his peers despite the classroom accommodations, Kesha tells Adam's mother that it is time to seek some advice from his family pediatrician. She also asks her to share any helpful information from the doctor with the staff so that they can assist Adam in any way possible.

DISCUSSION QUESTIONS

- Did Kesha do enough to protect the other children enrolled in the toddler classroom?
- Does the policy protect the needs of the biter and the other children enrolled in the class?
- Is there any acceptable reason that a childcare center should expel a toddler from the childcare program?

Chapter 7

A Sticky Situation with Confidentiality

Kathy believes that her childcare program has an extremely professional staff. She provides them with annual training on professionalism, confidentiality, the Federal Education Rights and Privacy Act, and how to work with families. After these annual trainings, each staff member signs an agreement that he or she understands the center policies on these topics and will adhere to the center policies and legal requirements.

Many of her staff members have been at her center for more than two years, and many of her families send multiple children through the early education program before each child begins kindergarten. Kathy knows that an extended commitment on the part of the families and the staff members is a sign of a positive learning environment for the children and a positive work environment for the staff. Kathy has had several staff members tell her that the center feels like a family. This is something that has always made Kathy very proud of her program.

Lately, while Kathy has been observing in the classrooms, she has noticed that teachers are not quite as guarded with children's personal information. The staff has always been very diligent about keeping medical information (e.g., food allergies or chronic illnesses) private, but they are sharing other details that concern Kathy.

For example, Ethan's mother came to pick him up one afternoon, and the teacher explained that Ethan had been scratched by a peer. She offered Ethan's mother an incident report to sign that concealed the name of the child who bit Ethan, and when Ethan's mother asked who had scratched him, the teacher told her that "a friend" had scratched him when they were arguing over a toy. They continued to have a casual conversation for a few minutes, and then Ethan's mother said that she was going to have a conversation with Ben's mother about how many times that Ben has scratched Ethan. The teacher then replied that Ben's mother was doing everything that she possibly could to work with the school to resolve the problem.

Last month, Kathy was observing in the two-year-old room during pickup time. Amelia came in to pick up her son, and the first question that she asked Ms. Kim, the teacher, was if her son had sat on the toilet during the day. Ms. Kim told her that he had not, and instantly, Amelia looked extremely disappointed. Amelia began looking around the room at the other children, and she asked Ms. Kim if all the other children in the classroom were toilet-trained yet.

Ms. Kim was desperately trying to encourage Amelia. She explained that although most of the children in the classroom were no longer wearing diapers, Mason and JaShae, along with Amelia's son, were still not toilet-trained. Then Ms. Kim began to explain that it frequently takes young boys longer to get toilet-trained than young girls.

After the mother left with her son, Kathy reminded Ms. Kim that she could share information with Amelia only about Amelia's own son, not the other children in the classroom. She asked Ms. Kim if she still had her handouts from the training in August, but Ms. Kim reminded Kathy that she had been hired in October.

Kathy meets with the parent booster club after school on Tuesdays, and although this week's meeting was supposed to be about fundraising, she found out quite a few details about her staff. Several of the parents approached Kathy about the little boy in the toddler room who has been scratching. All of the parents knew exactly which child it was, and they were asking questions about whether or not he should be in that classroom if he continued to scratch his peers.

As Kathy listened to their concerns, she found out that several of the parents had been in the classroom and seen Ben scratch another child. She also learned from several of the concerned parents that they had all been using Ms. Stephanie, one of the toddler teachers, as a babysitter on evenings or weekends, and the parents had been asking Stephanie questions about how frequently Ben scratched other children and what caused him to scratch his classmates.

Of course, it is only natural for parents to ask these questions to protect their children, but it seems that Stephanie may be giving personal information to parents about other children in the classroom. Kathy decides that this is an issue that she will need to address to the entire team of toddler teachers tomorrow during the school day.

Kathy wraps up the parent meeting and tells all of the families to have a nice evening. As she is cleaning up, Kathy notices that one parent has stayed behind. Ms. Sims asks Kathy if she can speak with her for just a moment, and then begins to tell Kathy that she had been out to eat with one of her friends the previous week at a restaurant, when she overheard something that bothered her.

Ms. Sims was at a local bar and grill, and she and her friend had been seated next to one of the school's preschool teachers, Ms. Lauren. Ms. Lauren politely said hello to Ms. Sims, and then they both sat down to enjoy their meals. During Ms. Sims's dinner, she could hear Lauren talking about one of the families in her classroom. She was telling her dinner partner that the Johnson family was in the middle of a divorce and that the parents were having a heated fight over primary custody.

Lauren went on to tell her friend that the mother should receive primary custody because she did not think that the father showed enough interest in his children. Ms. Sims was really shocked to hear Lauren say these things because she thought Lauren had always been the model of professionalism at the school.

It is obvious to Kathy that she must talk with the entire staff about protecting the confidentiality of the children and the families that they work with each day, but what does she need to change to help her staff be more aware of these policies?

REMINDERS

- Confidentiality does not only include medical information and academic progress of young children, but also their daily behavior in the classroom and developmental progress.
- Teaching staff must understand that confidentiality practices should be upheld during the school day, but they continue *outside* of the workday and even after the child is no longer in their care.
- All teachers must be trained on confidentiality and professional expectations in order to be held accountable for those practices.

Chapter 7

ACTION PLAN

Kathy decides to address some of these issues at the center-wide staff meeting. She begins by inviting a lawyer who serves on the advisory board to come and speak about what types of information each teacher is required to keep confidential in relationship to the children and families that they serve.

Instead of having each staff member sign a form that says he or she will agree to follow the center policies, Kathy and the assisting lawyer create a confidentiality agreement that outlines each requirement with a separate bullet point. This agreement incorporates the staff members' obligations inside and outside the workplace, and it includes confidentiality regarding photographs, email, and social media.

After the staff meeting, Kathy will begin to share this information with each new employee during the hiring process instead of waiting for the annual in-service training. Returning employees will still review this information each August prior to the start of the new school year.

Kathy also had some concerns about staff members babysitting for currently enrolled families in their free time. She knows that many of her staff members count on the extra money from babysitting to supplement their current paycheck, and she does not want to take away their extra income. At the same time, these staff members need to understand that their close relationships with the families still require professionalism.

Kathy decides to rewrite the policy on outside babysitting in the handbook. The policy now states that staff members have the freedom to babysit for currently enrolled families outside of work hours; however, each staff member is still required to uphold the confidentiality and professionalism required by his or her position. If he or she cannot meet those demands while babysitting for families during outside hours, then this could lead to the childcare program discontinuing his or her employment.

DISCUSSION QUESTIONS

- Did the staff meeting and training plan that Kathy implemented offer the staff the support they needed to understand the center policies?

- Did the new policies protect the rights of the families as well as the rights of the staff?
- Should Kathy allow staff members to babysit for currently enrolled families while they are employed at the center?

Chapter 8

A Sticky Situation with Parent Feedback

The Frederick Child Development Center has a suggestion box in the front lobby beside the front desk where families sign in their children each day. There have been some years that the suggestion box is rarely used, but this year the parents have been offering frequent suggestions. Natasha, the center owner, makes an effort to read through any suggestions that are left in the box by families, but not every suggestion is feasible for the center.

In the past couple of months parents have left suggestions for Natasha to lower the cost of tuition, extend the hours of operation to remain open later, and remove candy from the classroom treasure boxes as rewards. There has been one suggestion for families to choose whether or not their children should go outside on hot days. Another family has suggested that scholarships need to be offered to assist families with the cost of tuition and that the center remain open during inclement weather. Several families have requested that the family be allowed to suggest which classroom their children are placed in during the following school year. One family has asked that the school refrain from celebrating religious holidays, and another family has asked that the school have more holiday celebrations that include the families as well as the children.

Several of these suggestions conflict with one another, and other suggestions would place a financial strain on the child development center. However, the center is a small business, and it is in the best interest of the program to listen to the wants and needs of the families who are enrolled in the center. How can Natasha show the parents that she has made every effort to review their suggestions and select recommendations that are in the best interest of the program? How can Natasha review each suggestion objectively?

REMINDERS

- Although early childhood education programs are educational institutions, they are still small businesses. In order to attract families to the program, the center must be able to meet the needs of enough families to meet maximum enrollment. If families do not believe that the center is meeting their needs, then they are likely to leave and enroll in a program that will meet their needs.
- Most families enrolled in a childcare program understand that the center cannot meet *every* parent suggestion; however, each family appreciates having management listen to and acknowledge their concerns. Sometimes listening can be the greatest courtesy.
- Each childcare program has room for improvement, so it is essential for program management to find a way to accept constructive criticism. If it is challenging for the program owner or director to remain objective when reviewing potential suggestions, then perhaps a small group of leadership should review suggestions as a team.
- It is essential for families enrolled in a childcare center to offer feedback each year on the quality of care being offered. This allows the director or owner to see if the program is meeting the needs of the majority of families. In order to receive the most amount of feedback possible, all families need access to the evaluation process.
- Although most small businesses want to be as appealing as possible to potential clients, not every childcare program is the best fit for every potential family. For example, if the center has a mission statement that involves providing faith-based education, then many families may not agree with that style of education. It does not necessarily mean that the center needs to change in order to meet the needs of each family.

ACTION PLAN

Natasha is unsure how many families use the suggestion box, and she would like to see feedback from the entire parent population instead of just a small sample. Instead of simply using the suggestion box for parent comments, she decides that she will get a larger sample of parents to participate if she provides an annual evaluation to all of the families enrolled.

Natasha compiles a parent survey with thirty questions that include topics such as quality of teaching staff, consistency of teachers, school readiness, cost, facility, and school policies. At the end of the survey, Natasha includes a question that allows parents to comment on any other concerns about the program.

In order to have as many families as possible complete the survey, Natasha decides to send it out to the families by two different methods of communication: email and a hardcopy letter sent home in each child's school bag. Parents are asked in the email and the letter to complete the survey and submit it within a two-week period. Natasha also decides that some sort of incentive will improve the number of surveys turned in to the center, so she explains that every family that completes a survey and turns it back in will be entered into a drawing for 50 percent off of a week of tuition.

As the owner of the program, Natasha has invested a lot of time and effort into her program. She has designed it, and it can be very challenging to hear anyone suggest that the program has flaws. At the same time, it is essential to take time each year to reflect on ways to improve the center.

Natasha decides to ask the program director, two veteran teachers, and the chair of the parent booster committee to review the parent evaluations with her to see if any suggestions are feasible and will be in the best interest of the children. Natasha does explain to the other members of the committee that at this time the center does not have the ability to cut the cost of tuition or to offer scholarships. She shows each committee member a copy of the school budget, including income and expenses, and demonstrates that all anticipated tuition income is needed this year to meet the requirements of the budget.

The committee reviews the parent feedback that includes school policies, curriculum, and health and safety policies. The committee agrees that it would be in the best interest of the children to remove candy and other sugary treats from the classroom treasure boxes. The committee decides to reinforce the policy that all holidays (of different origins) will be celebrated in the classrooms in a way to teach multiculturalism and social studies. The committee also decides that parents may suggest the preschool teacher that they would like their children to have the following school year, but the family must understand that the owner and director will make the best decision for all of the children involved.

Natasha will share the results of the family survey at the next parent education night. Also, Ms. Riley, the chair of the parent booster committee, will share the results of the parent evaluations and a summary of the committee decisions at the next parent booster meeting.

DISCUSSION QUESTIONS

- Did Natasha find the best way to collect parent feedback at her center?
- What are the benefits of reviewing parent feedback each year?
- What is the best method to show parents that you are listening to their concerns if the center is unable to change the center policy at that time?
- How does an owner/director decide if the center should change a policy or if the family should look for a center that better meets their needs?

Chapter 9

A Sticky Situation with Staff Gossip

Erika supervises forty-seven staff members, including classroom teaching staff, support staff, and the administrative team members, as the director of the Littleton Early Learning Center (Littleton ELC). The lead teacher and the assistant teacher in each classroom spend almost six and a half hours a day together. Although most of the staff members primarily spend time with just the teachers in their classroom, the staff as a whole usually gets along very well. Currently, Erika schedules whole staff meetings every three months and then communicates with the staff by email in between those meetings.

The center is set up on a long hallway with all of the classrooms breaking off of the main wing. At the front of the building are the administrative office, the staff breakroom, and the public restrooms. The kitchen is at the end of the hallway. There are two playgrounds, one for infants and toddlers and one for preschool children. The playgrounds are on the opposite sides of the building, and only the infant-toddler playground is visible from the office. The hallway of classrooms makes it possible for an administrator to see the length of the hallway at one time, but the building is not set up for the teachers of different classrooms to collaborate. Ms. Emma is the lead preschool teacher in preschool classroom A, and her assistant teacher is Ms. Virna. Ms. Angie is the lead preschool teacher in preschool classroom B, and her assistant teacher is Ms. Nikki. Ms. Melanie and Ms. Deonne are co-teachers in the oldest toddler classroom. Ms. Lauren and Ms. Toby are co-teachers in the youngest toddler classroom.

Lately, rumors seem to be circulating in the building more than usual. Ms. Emma, a preschool teacher, asked to speak with Erika last week, and she told Erika that her assistant teacher has been spreading gossip about her. Ms. Emma said that several of the other teachers have asked when she is leaving her lead teacher position, and when she asked them where they heard that, they said that her assistant teacher had already said that she is applying for her position when Emma leaves.

Erika asked Ms. Emma if she has been considering leaving Littleton ELC, and Ms. Emma said that she had considered it months ago. Erika told Ms. Emma that she needs to speak directly to Ms. Virna and let her know that Emma is no longer considering leaving the center. She stressed to Emma that in order to prevent the spread of gossip, she needs to have direct conversations with her coworkers.

A few days later, Angie stopped Erika in the hallway and said that she felt uncomfortable around her assistant teacher. She said that she has noticed that Nikki stops talking to other teachers as soon as Angie approaches her. Erika asked Angie if she had spoken with Nikki about her concerns. She said that she didn't want to make the situation worse. She felt like Nikki was already using an "icy" tone of voice, and when Angie was in the teacher work room on Tuesday she heard someone say that Nikki wanted to transfer to a different classroom.

Erika told Angie that she needed to have a conversation with Nikki and ask her if she feels like there is a problem in the classroom. If she is uncomfortable having this conversation alone, then Erika is happy to mediate, but it is essential that Angie and Nikki talk to one another instead of other teachers in the building.

Then yesterday Lauren came down to Erika's office and said that she saw Melanie post a comment on her social media account about a coworker stabbing her in the back. Erika thanked Lauren for letting her know this information, and then she asked Melanie to come to her office to speak with her in private.

Erika began by explaining to Melanie that it is very unprofessional to post negative comments about her workplace on social media. This type of unprofessional behavior can cause someone to lose a job or prevent him or her from being considered for a position in the future. After discussing the social media policy, Erika asked her why she was upset with her coworker.

Melanie began to explain how Toby told her that Melanie's co-teacher, Deonne, was telling several parents that Melanie was unorganized and not recording the infants' feeding and diapering schedule accurately. Melanie was hurt by these comments, and she posted the comments on social media even before she had time to speak with Deonne.

Once again, Erika told Melanie to speak directly with Deonne to see what she said to the parents. If Deonne is frustrated with Melanie's organizational skills, then Melanie needs to know that information. It is also possible that Toby did not hear the conversation correctly, and he misinterpreted what Deonne told the families.

Erika needs to find a way to encourage the staff to communicate with one another instead of gossiping to other staff members when there is a conflict. What should she do to improve staff relationships?

REMINDERS

- It is essential for the administrative team to reinforce and model a direct communication method whenever there is conflict between staff members or between parents and staff.
- When gossip is presented to management, the administrators must encourage each staff member to have open and honest conversations to confront the rumor instead of continuing to circulate the gossip.
- Staff members are the greatest asset to any early childhood program. If staff members are not getting along, the administration needs to find a way to encourage staff and develop stronger relationships.

ACTION PLAN

Erika knows that with a staff of forty-seven people, she is always going to have some amount of gossip; however, she does believe that the center can improve the current staff climate. She begins by scheduling a meeting with the rest of the administrative team. The management team believes that a great deal of the gossip is stemming from the fact that not all of the staff members know each other. They brainstorm ways to improve the sense of community at the center.

In four weeks the center will be closed for professional development, so the administrators decide that they would like to focus the training on team building and staff cooperation. Shawna, the assistant director, has volunteered to find a regional speaker who focuses on this topic. Alex, the finance director, also suggests that Erika add an additional staff meeting in the next quarter so that the staff members have another opportunity to spend time with one another and get to know each other better. Erika offers to reach out to the parent advisory board to see if they will organize a staff dinner for that night from the parents since that is not currently on the staff calendar.

Erika asks that each member of the management team be diligent to model a direct approach to answering questions and eliminating gossip. If a staff member comes to them with a concern or a rumor, encourage that person first to speak with the person with whom he or she has a conflict. If the two staff members are uncomfortable speaking with one another, then a member of the management team can mediate, but only after the two have attempted to work out the disagreement on their own first. Erika will speak about direct communication at the next staff meeting and explain to all staff members that this is a key element of professionalism.

DISCUSSION QUESTIONS

- Did Erika do enough to reduce the amount of gossip in her childcare program?
- How can focusing on staff relationships and team building help to eliminate this problem in the center?
- If the problem continues to persist, should it become a disciplinary issue?

Chapter 10

A Sticky Situation with Social Media

John manages a large childcare program, and currently there is no written policy about using social media. During new staff orientation, each teacher is given information about the school's confidentiality policy, and the entire staff is retrained on this policy every August before the start of the new school year. John knows that most of his staff members are in contact with one another on social media, and many of the staff members communicate with parents that way also. He has never worried about the information that is being shared by staff members on social media because of the confidentiality and professionalism training that his staff receive regularly.

On Wednesday, Ms. Waters asks to speak with John in his office. She tells him that her son's teacher, Ms. Amber, has been making a lot of comments on social media about how she doesn't want to go to work, how exhausted she is, and how she doesn't get along with the co-teachers in her classroom. Ms. Waters is worried about Ms. Amber's ability to do her job well, and she would like her son to be moved to a different classroom.

John is surprised by this information, but he assures Ms. Waters that he is going to look into the problem. He politely asks her to be patient and allow her son to stay in his current classroom while he takes some time to investigate.

John pulls up Ms. Amber's social media page, and he begins to scroll through the posts. There is nothing said about a child or even a specific coworker. She repeatedly complains about her job without using the name of the center; however, she does list the center as her employer under her personal information. John can easily see why Ms. Waters is upset. The information on the teacher's social media account makes it appear that Ms. Amber is very unhappy at her job.

On Thursday, John asks Ms. Amber to come to his office and speak with him. Without saying anything about her social media account, John tells Ms. Amber that he wants to know how she is doing in the classroom and if she feels like it is a good fit for her. She says that she really likes her job, even though it is exhausting at times.

After she reassures John that she enjoys her job, he asks her why she would post so many complaints about her job on social media if she enjoys doing it. Ms. Amber is taken aback that John has seen her page, but she begins to explain that she uses her page as a way to unwind at the end of the day and nothing on it should be taken too seriously.

John explains to her that a parent came to him with concerns because the teacher's post seemed to indicate that she did not like the job and was unhappy. Ms. Amber stated that she had never thought about how the parents might read into one of her posts when they saw it. She told John that she was friends with eight or nine of the parents in her classroom. One of the families frequently asked her to babysit on evenings and weekends. John asked Ms. Amber to refrain from writing negative posts about her job or the center on her page in the future.

Over the weekend, John decided to review posts of other center employees who had the social media pages visible to the public. He found that many of his employees were posting information about their jobs, both positive and negative. One employee even wrote a post about how her boss was completely unreasonable.

John noticed that several of his younger employees were using foul language on their social media pages and posting inappropriate pictures as well. When he looked more closely at their pages, John realized that those same employees were also friends with parents in their classrooms. Finally, John saw a post of an employee at a mall shopping with a friend the previous week on that same day that the employee had called in sick to work.

John did not find any pictures of children or the center posted on someone's page, so it comforted him to know that some of the training on confidentiality was working. Most of the posts that concerned John had more to do with professionalism than confidentiality. It worried

John that his staff did not understand the effects of posting these types of pictures of themselves or using this type of negativity on a public forum. It is also a concern that parents may believe that level of professionalism is acceptable at John's childcare program. John knew that he needed to implement some type of staff training and create a social media policy for the center that protects both the staff members and the program as a whole.

REMINDERS

- Although every individual has the right to freedom of speech (including in the digital world), when you use that freedom you may incur its consequences. Those consequences can include losing the trust of those around you or losing your job.
- The privacy of children, their families, and coworkers must be honored at all times.
- Information placed on social media can travel quickly, and many people outside your normal circle will view that information. It is easy for an employee to damage his or her career permanently if he or she is careless online.
- The program must have a plan in place to protect itself if an employee provides negative information about the program in a public forum.

ACTION PLAN

John decides to create a social media policy for the program. After board approval, his new policy states that:

- Employees may not share confidential information about children, the children's families, or coworkers on social media.
- The center does not tolerate discrimination (including age, sex, race, color, creed, religion, ethnicity, sexual orientation, gender identity, national origin, citizenship, disability, or marital status or any other legally recognized protected basis under federal, state, or local laws, regulations or ordinances), so do not post information that would go against program values.

- Never post any information about the legal status or financial viability of the program.
- Protect yourself. Be extremely careful about what personal information you share online. It may have long-term effects on your career or personal life.
- Do not post anything that belongs to another person. Let families and coworkers share their own stories.
- Do not communicate with currently enrolled families on social media if you cannot demonstrate your professionalism at all times.
- Failure to follow the social media policy could lead to disciplinary action or termination of employment.

After the new policy and the employee handbook are written, John schedules a mandatory staff meeting to review the content with every employee. He asks the center's lawyer to come and discuss the legal implications of the policy, but he also invites a career counselor from the local university to come and speak about the effects that social media can have on the hiring process. John wants his younger staff members to understand how important it is to protect themselves on social media.

At the end of the meeting he explains that employees who do not follow the social media policy will be subject to the center's three-step disciplinary action process, just like other policies in the employee handbook. After the employees have heard the new policy, they must sign the employee handbook agreement that they understand the employee handbook policies and they will adhere to them.

DISCUSSION QUESTIONS

- Should John allow the employees to continue to stay in contact with current families on social media?
- Is his new social media policy too strict? Or is it necessary to cover each of the points listed in his policy?
- Would you have handled this situation in a different manner?

Chapter 11

A Sticky Situation with Staff Playground Behavior

Sugar and Spice Childcare has two separate playgrounds, one for infants and toddlers and one for preschool students. Sharee, the director, will allow one or two classrooms to go out to the playground at a time, but neither playground is designed for all of the students to access the playground at once. The infant and toddler playground has a couple of climbing structures appropriate for young children, a water table, a pretend play house, and several riding toys. The preschool playground has a large climbing structure with slides and a climbing wall, a pretend play house, a sand box, a water table, and a path for riding toys. There is a bench for adult seating on each playground at the front of the outdoor area. Although there are surveillance cameras in each classroom, there is currently not a camera on either playground. Each playground has a privacy fence that encloses the play area. The playgrounds are both large and L-shaped, so the teachers cannot see the entire playground at one time unless they stand in the middle corner.

When Sharee is in her office, she cannot see the playground areas, so during the day she may not get to view the children during outdoor play unless she purposely goes out to the playground. Now that spring temperatures are getting warmer, the classrooms have really been enjoying their outdoor time each day. The center's accreditation requires that every classroom spends thirty minutes outside for gross motor play twice daily. Because only one or two classrooms can be out on the playground at the same time, it is difficult for any classroom to spend more than an hour a day outside. Moreover, each classroom must complete its daily lesson plans and curriculum, so an hour of outdoor gross motor time is all the schedule will allow.

   The parent handbook states that all classrooms will go outside twice daily unless there are extreme weather conditions (thunderstorm advisory, tornado watch, heat advisory, etc.). About a month ago, Sharee walked past the two-year-olds classroom during their assigned playground time and saw that the entire class was inside playing. Sharee asked the teacher, Ms. Jessica, to come to her office at the end of the shift. When Ms. Jessica arrived in her office, Sharee asked her why she had not taken her classroom outside during their playground time. Ms. Jessica said that the temperature was too hot for the young children, and she thought it would be better for them to play inside. Sharee said that the temperature outside was only in the low eighties, so the children should be fine to go outside and play as long as they were all using their sunscreen. Ms. Jessica also mentioned that the temperature had risen higher than she had anticipated, and Sharee noticed that Jessica was wearing long pants and long-sleeved shirt. Sharee reminded her that unless there are extreme weather conditions Jessica must take her students outside to play twice a day.

   The incident with Jessica made Sharee think that maybe she should watch the playground more closely to make sure that all the children were getting enough outdoor playtime. She decided to observe one of the preschool classrooms the next day during outdoor playtime. Sharee watched from the inside door of the playground for twenty minutes, and she saw that the preschool teachers sat on the bench at the front of the playground the entire time she observed the classroom. There was no way that the teachers could see every child on the playground while seated on the bench due to the shape of the playground. After twenty minutes, Sharee walked out to the bench and asked the teachers how many children they had in attendance. Both teachers immediately looked at the sign-in sheet to count how many children had come to school today. Sharee told both teachers that they need to know the number of students on the playground without looking at the list and that they should be walking around the playground observing the students and counting students to make sure that all students are present. One of the teachers made a comment that she just needed to sit down for a while because her feet were hurting. Sharee looked down and saw that the teacher was wearing high-heeled sandals on the playground. Sharee reminded her to wear more appropriate footwear on the playground and then her feet would not hurt.

For several days, Sharee made a point of walking past the playground as every class took their outdoor play time. She noticed that most teachers sat by the benches or stood close to them to talk to each other. The teachers were not moving around the playground to see all the children, and the teachers were not interacting with the children as they played. Each time Sharee saw these behaviors, she stopped what she was doing to go and remind the teachers about the playground behavior. Then on a Wednesday afternoon, a parent came to Sharee with a concern about the playground. Mrs. Wilder told Sharee that the teachers do not seem engaged with the children on the playground, and at times, it does not seem like they are even supervising them. Sharee needs to change the behavior of the staff on the playground. What does she need to do to provide the best possible childcare for the children in her program?

REMINDERS

- Some of the greatest tools that a director can possess are personal relationships with the staff members. If the staff members trust and respect the director, then the staff members are much more likely to accept suggestions and even criticism from the director.
- One of the most effective methods for training staff members is having a director or veteran teacher model the desired behavior in the classroom with the children so that other staff members can see a concrete example of what is expected.
- When teachers do not properly supervise a playground, it can be a health and safety risk to the children. Many children are accidently injured on the playground when climbing, riding toys, or playing rough with other children.
- It is essential that all teachers know the number of children present in the classroom at all times, indoors and outdoors. When a teacher does not know how many children are present on the playground, it is possible to leave a child on the playground when the rest of the classroom lines up to go inside.
- A teacher should never be sitting and resting on the playground. It is the teacher's job to roam the playground and supervise all children.

It is also important for teachers to participate in conversations and participate in play with the children.
- A teacher must wear clothing to work that allows him or her to complete the assigned job responsibilities. A classroom of young children should never lose outdoor playground time because the teacher is not dressed appropriately for the weather or to move freely around the playground.

ACTION PLAN

After reviewing the details of the playground situation, Sharee decided that some of the staff members may not understand the best safety procedures for the playground. She decides that modeling the appropriate playground behavior may be the best place to start, so she looks at her calendar and blocks off every afternoon for the next week. Sharee will rotate between the infant and toddler playground and the preschool playground each afternoon and stay outside as each classroom rotates through outdoor playtime. While she models her playground behavior, Sharee makes sure that she is wearing clothing that allows her to do her job on the playground, and she also makes an effort to station herself in an area of the playground that allows her to see all of the children at one time. While she is on the playground, Sharee does talk to the other staff members, but her conversations are about what is going on with the children on the playground. Sharee also models appropriate conversations with the children, asking them questions about their outdoor play activities. As each classroom arrives on the playground and lines up to go inside, Sharee counts the number of children present.

After a week of modeling these habits on both playgrounds, Sharee decides to take a step back and watch the playground from inside the building to see if the teacher behaviors have changed. Although one or two teachers are making more of an effort to walk around the playground and interact with all the children, most of the teachers are still sitting on the bench at the front of the playground and talking to one another. Sharee realizes that she needs to take a different approach to ensure safety on the playground.

She does not want to have adult seating on the playground. Sharee decides to make an appointment to speak to the owner about removing the teachers' bench from the playground. Without a location to sit, she believes that the teachers would be more likely to walk around the playground. When Sharee gets the opportunity to speak with the center owner, she also asks if it is possible to add an observation camera to each playground for accountability. The owner agrees to both requests.

Sharee schedules a mandatory staff meeting for a Tuesday evening after the center is closed so that all staff members are able to attend. She begins by talking about the importance of knowing how many children are present in their classroom and continually taking a head count throughout the school day. Sharee tells the staff that during the next two weeks she will be stopping by each classroom repeatedly to ask about the number of children present, and she expects teachers to know that number without looking at the sign-in sheet.

The second topic on the agenda at the staff meeting is employee dress code. She reviews the policy on dress code from the employee handbook, but next she talks about each employee's job expectations and how those expectations affect their attire. All employees should be able to chase after a child on the playground if necessary. All employees should be able to lift a child when needed. All employees should be dressed to go outside each day, whether it is summer or winter.

Finally, Sharee talks to the staff about how to supervise the children properly on the playground. When there are multiple teachers on the playground, they should be spaced out to be closer to all children. Since Sugar and Spice Childcare has the two L-shaped playgrounds, it is impossible for employees to sit at the front of the playground and see the entire play area. Teachers need to think about how to position themselves to see the most children and which areas need the most teacher assistance. Also, the teachers are responsible for watching the children on the playground, not for talking to one another on the playground.

After Sharee has covered these three agenda items, she explains to the staff that the benches are going to be removed from both playgrounds. She also lets them know, for safety reasons, the owner will be placing an observation camera on both playgrounds so that Sharee can make sure there is appropriate supervision at all times on the playground. If teachers do not properly supervise the playground, then the administration team will use the employee redirection plan written in the staff handbook. Teachers will initially be given a verbal warning if they are not supervising children on the playground, but if they continue to provide poor supervision, the director will write a corrective action plan for the staff members. During the time that the corrective action plan is in place, the staff member will be supervised more closely. If the employee fails to meet the requirements of the corrective action plan, then it could lead to termination.

Sharee stressed that these steps might seem significant for simple problems on the playground; however, a lack of supervision is a major health and safety concern when caring for young children. Sharee does not want the playground behavior of the adults to result in one of the children sustaining an injury or being left alone on the playground. At the end of the staff meeting, Sharee has each employee sign a statement saying that he or she understands the information from the staff meeting and will follow the center policies.

DISCUSSION QUESTIONS

- Did Sharee overreact to the problems on the playground, or did she implement appropriate changes to ensure safety?
- How do you think that the staff will respond to the changes that Sharee made?
- Why is it essential for children to have a safe outdoor environment to play in each day?

Chapter 12

A Sticky Situation with Parent Behavior

The Bakersfield Preschool Center is a close-knit community. Jose, the director, has been at the center for over eight years, and most of his staff members have been at the center for over two years. He even has staff members who have been teaching at the preschool close to fifteen years. There is always a waiting list for the preschool, and many of the families enrolled at the center have had multiple children go through the preschool program and graduate. Family events at the Bakersfield Preschool are always successful because the families love participating and spending time with one another. There is a strong sense of community interaction between the staff and families.

Although most of the families enrolled in the program already know each other, this year a new family enrolled at the preschool after moving to Bakersfield from out of state. Mr. and Mrs. Lamar were in town only for a few months before they told Jose that they would be getting a divorce. They wanted Jose and their son's teachers to let them know if James, their son, did not seem to be adjusting well to his new living arrangements.

Mr. Lamar was going to have primary custody, and Mrs. Lamar would see James every other weekend. If Mr. Lamar needs to travel out of town, then Mrs. Lamar would be responsible for James during those trips. Both parents would remain on the pickup list and remain the primary contacts on James's emergency forms. Mr. Lamar's mother and father would also remain on the pickup list, as well as Mrs. Lamar's sister.

Jose thanked both parents for trusting this information with the preschool program, and he encouraged them to contact himself or the teachers if they had any concerns about how James was dealing with the separation.

Although James seemed to be doing well with his new living arrangements, Mr. and Ms. Lamar did not seem to be handling their own situations with as much grace. One Friday afternoon Ms. Lamar came to pick James up from school, and James was wearing an outfit that she did not recognize. The teacher explained that James had had an accident that day on the way to the toilet and soiled his clothes. The teacher found a clean outfit for James to wear home in the school's supply of extra clothing, and the school just asks the family to wash the outfit and bring it back in to the program on Monday.

Ms. Lamar cursed out loud in the classroom. The teacher asked Ms. Lamar to step out of the classroom, and Jose escorted her to the administrative office. He reminded Ms. Lamar that young children do not need to hear that kind of language. He also explained that the teachers are working hard to take care of the children in their classrooms, and the school asks that all families use respectful language when speaking to the preschool staff.

Two weeks later when it was Ms. Lamar's turn to pick up James on Friday afternoon, she was late to pick him up from school. The preschool program closes each day at 6:00 p.m. At 6:05 p.m., when no one had arrived to pick up James from school, the teacher began calling the numbers on James's emergency contact list. She called Ms. Lamar first because James said that his mommy was picking him up from school; however, when she did not answer, the teacher called Mr. Lamar next. Mr. Lamar was extremely upset that his ex-wife did not pick up James, and he said that he would arrive at the school within five minutes.

As Mr. Lamar pulled away from the school with James, Ms. Lamar arrived at the preschool program. She was very upset that the teacher allowed James's father to pick up James from school when it was her day to be with him. Ms. Lamar spoke very harshly to the teacher, but the teacher reminded Ms. Lamar that both parents are allowed to pick up James from childcare and it is not her job to interfere with a child's legal guardian's custody rights.

Three weeks later, Mr. Lamar called and scheduled a meeting with Jose. Mr. Lamar explained that he was now seeking full custody of his son because his ex-wife was being very irresponsible regarding James's care. He asked Jose to take Ms. Lamar off the emergency contact list. Jose explained he could not remove Ms. Lamar from any of the school documents until he saw a court document that terminated her parental rights. Mr. Lamar told Jose that he would bring in those documents as soon as he received them.

Several weeks later, Mr. Lamar submitted new court documents to Jose stating that Mr. Lamar had full custody of James, and Ms. Lamar did not have visitation rights. Jose informed the teachers that Ms. Lamar no longer had legal rights to pick up her son from school. He also asked Mr. Lamar to update all of the emergency forms and the list of adults allowed to leave school property with James.

Since this was such a sensitive topic, Jose asked the teachers to let him know how James was coping with all of these changes. If James began having a difficult time with transitions or relating to the other children in the classroom, Jose asked the teachers to let him know immediately.

James continued to do well despite all of the changes in his life, but more concerns seemed to surface with his parents. Last month, during evening dismissal, Mr. Lamar came to school to pick up James. About ten minutes after James and Mr. Lamar left the building, another parent came into the office and said that two adults were in the parking lot yelling at each other in front of a playground full of children.

Jose walked outside to find Mr. Lamar and Ms. Lamar screaming at one another with James standing beside them watching. There was also a classroom full of preschool students on the playground watching the family. The preschool teachers were trying to quickly get the children in a line to walk back into the building.

As Jose approached the arguing adults, Ms. Lamar attempted to punch Mr. Lamar in the face. Jose told one of the preschool teachers to call the police and report a domestic dispute on the preschool property. Then he walked closer to James's mother and father and told them that they were not allowed to behave this way on the preschool property. Jose suggested that he take James back inside to get a drink with his friends while his father and mother calm down. Both adults agreed, and James went inside with Jose. Just as all the children were back inside the building, two police officers arrived on the property and began to speak with Mr. Lamar and Ms. Lamar.

This situation completely took Jose and his staff by surprise. They never anticipated a family enrolled in their program would act this way at the preschool. Did Jose and his staff handle this situation in the best possible way for James? How should they handle this type of situation if it were to ever occur again?

REMINDERS

- The most important job of a childcare program is to protect the health and safety of the children. This includes the physical health and safety of the children and the emotional health of the children, too.
- Although a childcare provider is an important caregiver for a child, nothing can diminish the role of a parent. Unless a parent has legally lost the right to be the primary caregiver (with documentation that supports that loss), then a childcare provider may not interfere in a custody agreement.
- If an adult behaves inappropriately in the childcare program, then the center has the right to ask the adult to leave the center. If an adult is putting himself or herself at risk or threatening the safety of another child or adult, then it is appropriate to call the police to remove that threat from the center's property.
- A small business, like a childcare program, has the right to refuse service to an individual who does not adhere to the program policies. Each childcare program should outline unacceptable adult behavior in its family handbook.

ACTION PLAN

After the incident with James's mother and father, Jose scheduled a mandatory staff meeting to talk with the staff about what happened. In the meeting he reviewed these key points:

- If an adult uses inappropriate language or behavior on center property, the staff members need to ask the adult to stop and remind him or her that children are present. If the adult does not refrain, then the person should be asked to leave the property.
- If an adult on the property (classrooms or playground) behaves in a way that could harm the children or the staff, it is top priority to

remove the children from any potential danger. After the children are safe, the staff members need to contact police immediately.
- Staff members must be diligent in reviewing the list of approved adults who are authorized to pick up a child from the center. If an adult comes to pick up a child who is not on the list, it is the staff members' duty to contact the parents to let them know that the center does not have written permission to release the child to the adult.
- Court documents regarding custody must be followed. If there is a custody dispute between parents, the center must have a copy of the legal court document stating the legal caregivers.

Jose stressed to each staff member that these policies need to be followed regardless of which staff members are onsite. Even if he is not here, the person in charge must follow these policies adamantly to ensure safety of every staff member and child.

DISCUSSION QUESTIONS

- What type of adult behavior is inappropriate on the premises of a childcare program?
- Did Jose give his staff enough information about how to handle any future disruptions on school property?
- As the center director, did Jose handle the custody dispute between Mr. Lamar and Ms. Lamar appropriately?

Chapter 13

A Sticky Situation with Annual Evaluations

Lucy has been the director of Baby Bundles Childcare for seven and a half years, and she a strong relationship with her staff members. In the past, when she had a staff member who was not following center policy, Lucy asked the staff member to speak with her privately in her office to find a way to address the concern. When staff members were doing what they were supposed to do, they rarely heard any input from Lucy. Two years ago, Baby Bundles became accredited by the state QRS (quality rating system), and the new accreditation required each employee to have an annual evaluation each year at the anniversary of the staff member's hire date.

 This change in operation was so intimidating to the staff that Lucy attempted to make the evaluations as nonthreatening as possible. During the first year that she used the evaluation with the staff, she gave everyone a glowing review, even when they had areas that needed improvement. Since everyone's evaluations are conducted at different points in the year, based on the hire date, Lucy never found a time period that she felt was appropriate to start conducting accurate evaluations. After two years with this system, there is an established culture at the childcare center that everyone passes their evaluation even if their performance is lacking.

 Lucy has also been disappointed that the evaluation meeting is one-sided. Right now, the teachers listen to Lucy read the evaluation that she has filled out, but they do not comment on their own performance or give feedback on their past year of work at Baby Bundles. Lucy would like to re-create the evaluation process, but she is afraid that her staff members will all be upset if they do not receive perfect evaluations.

REMINDERS

- When a center director looks at changing a policy with which all staff members are comfortable, it is essential to get staff to "buy-in" to make the new policy successful.
- The purpose of an annual evaluation is to identify both strengths and weaknesses of each employee and to use that information to set goals for the upcoming year. No staff member is perfect, so each person should have areas to improve upon during the program year.
- Staff members should be offered some type of incentive to meet their upcoming goals. If the center can offer a monetary incentive, that is fabulous, but most centers must look for alternative incentives to inspire employees.
- Staff members who show continued poor performance may not receive the same incentives that more capable staff members receive.
- Staff members need to utilize the annual evaluation to reflect on their own performance and use the time with the administrator to discuss their own concerns.

ACTION PLAN

Since Lucy has several veteran members of the staff who are respected by the other teachers, she decides to invite them to a discussion about the annual evaluations to brainstorm the best way to improve the process. The experienced staff members agree that the evaluations are ineffective, and they believe that Lucy could use them in a more beneficial way. One of the teachers suggests that brand-new teachers should not wait a full year for an evaluation. Since the more experienced teachers are usually called on to train the new staff, they suggest that new staff receive a primary evaluation at the end of the training period.

Ms. Renee says that her daughter's childcare program has a ninety-day probationary period for training new staff members. At the end of the probationary period, the staff member receives an evaluation that can either recommend the teacher for permanent hire or end the teacher's employment without the teacher being fired. Ms. Renee also says that the supervising teacher who trains the new staff member gets to offer a recommendation for the evaluation. Also, during the initial ninety days, new staff members may not schedule vacation so that they have every opportunity to receive training and develop relationships with the children and the staff.

Mr. George suggests an evaluation with a point-based system. The teachers can be rated on each item on a 1 to 5 scale. If the staff member breaks a certain point level, then he or she is eligible for an annual raise. If the staff member does not achieve that point level, then he thinks that the teacher needs to work harder during the next year to achieve a raise. On a 1 to 5 scale, George says that employees who receive mostly 1s and 2s should not receive a raise, but if they receive scores of average or above average then they should receive a raise.

Lucy tells the staff members that she would like the evaluation process to be a little more reflective for the teaching staff. Ms. Sarah suggests that before they scheduled an evaluation both the teacher and the director fill out the evaluation about the past year's performance. Sarah says that the teachers often ask the parents to do this before conferences to make sure that parents think about their child's development before they discuss it with the teachers. Then if there are areas of disagreement, the teacher and Lucy can discuss the differences.

After talking with the teachers, Lucy creates a performance evaluation that focuses on the areas of professionalism and attendance, family engagement, coworker relationships, and classroom environment. Each item in these four areas will be rated on a 1 to 5 scale.

1 = poor performance
2 = occasional poor performance
3 = satisfactory performance
4 = above average performance
5 = exceptional performance

The tool also has a section that discusses the teachers' greatest strengths and areas for improvement. For the twenty-four individual items on the tool, the teacher must receive a score of 60 out of a possible 120 to earn a raise for the upcoming program year.

After Lucy creates the evaluation, she meets with Renee, George, and Sarah one more time. She has the teachers look at the expectations on the evaluation compared to the teachers' job descriptions to make sure that the evaluation is fair. The teachers find a few places where they want to change the wording of an evaluation item, but overall, they like the new evaluation. Lucy tells them that she wants to discuss the evaluation at the next staff meeting. She is going to open up the topic of the evaluation and the need for changing it, but she would then like for Renee, George, and Sarah to talk about the suggestions they made and the reason for those suggestions. After the staff meeting, Lucy will begin using the new evaluation for each annual performance review. For annual reviews, she will give the teacher a copy of the evaluation one week in advance of the meeting so that he or she can do a self-evaluation.

Lucy is also going to begin the ninety-day evaluation for each new employee hired. When the employee begins at Baby Bundles Childcare he or she will be told about the ninety-day probationary period for training. At the end of the training window, the teacher mentor and the director will complete the evaluation to recommend for hire. New staff members will be told that they cannot request vacation time until after the training period is complete.

DISCUSSION QUESTIONS

- What are the benefits of asking the teachers to help create the annual evaluation?
- Did the staff member create a fair evaluation system?
- Do you think that the other staff members will accept the new evaluation system when it is presented by their coworkers?

Chapter 14

A Sticky Situation with an Advisory Board

Melissa is the director of a nonprofit childcare program for children ages 5 and under. Her center, Children's Place Childcare, has been open for twenty-three years, and it was initially founded by a group of community members who wanted to provide high-quality childcare at a reasonable cost for working families. The center is still owned by the advisory board, and there are currently twelve board members. Each term on the board is a three-year appointment, and new board members are selected each spring by a nomination committee. There is no limit to how many terms a board member may serve on the Children's Place advisory board, but about half of the board members rotate off of the board after one or two terms. There are several board members who have served for a long tenure, and one of the founding board members is still on the board today.

   The board members come from very diverse backgrounds. Some of the members developed an interest in serving on the board when their own children were enrolled in the childcare program, but most members were recruited from the community by other board members. The members typically do not have a background in education. Most of the members are business owners, bankers, marketing executives, lawyers, or civic leaders. They have been encouraged to participate because of their business background or their experience on other nonprofit advisory boards in the community. As the director, Melissa is an ex-officio member of the board and is regarded as the education specialist on the committee.

The advisory board's job is to supervise the director position; approve the annual budget; set the mission statement of the program; improve community partnerships; and serve on committees, including daily operations, marketing, finance, and facility management. The executive board consists of four members: the board president, the past president, the treasurer, and the secretary. The executive board members are extremely involved with Children's Place, and they volunteer many more hours than the other board members, particularly the president and the treasurer. Typically, the board members do not interact with the families enrolled in the program, except for those families who volunteer to assist with community fund-raising.

As director, Melissa is responsible for making most of the daily business decisions like hiring, scheduling, and collecting tuition. Melissa is also the chair of the staff committee that selects and approves curriculum. Recently the board members have been taking more of an interest in these areas of operation. When a job opening has been posted, board members have been making recommendations on whom they would like Melissa to hire.

Unfortunately, they have been recommending potential candidates who do not have the education requirements to meet the center's accreditation requirements. Also, the board has been reviewing the current student-to-teacher ratios in the classroom, and they have been asking Melissa if it would be possible to increase the number of students in each classroom. Again, this change would not meet the requirements of the program's accreditation.

Since the board members are Melissa's supervisors, she does not want to reject their suggestions, but she does need to find a way to explain the importance of why educational background and student-to-teacher ratio are essential to the accreditation process and essential to the original mission of the program. How can she approach her board with this information?

REMINDERS

- An advisory board can be a huge asset to a program director because the board members can have areas of expertise with which the director has no education or experience.

- An effective advisory board can also keep the integrity of the program over a long period of time since staff members can continue to come and go. The board prevents a single director from changing the mission of the program and provides accountability to the staff.
- Since board members may not have knowledge about early childhood education, it is essential to provide these volunteers with training on what the program offers to children and families.
- It is very beneficial for board members to see how the early education directly benefits the families by hearing the stories of enrolled families and see what is done in the program's classroom.

ACTION PLAN

Melissa decides to ask the board president if she can meet with the executive board to discuss the center's mission, and she asks a currently enrolled family to come for the first fifteen minutes of the meeting to tell their story about how Children's Place has benefitted their family situation. After the family talks about how safe they feel leaving their eighteen-month-old daughter with teachers who love her, Melissa explains to the board that these stories are the foundation of Children's Place Childcare. She would like to include a parent moment at the beginning of each board meeting so that board members can hear real-life stories about the children in the program. The executive board eagerly agrees that this would be an excellent way to start off each business meeting.

Melissa then begins to talk about the benefits of being an accredited early childhood education program and the requirements of that program, comparing those benefits and requirements to the mission statement at every opportunity. She thanks the executive board for all of the hours they have volunteered and assisted her with budgets, marketing campaigns, and fund-raising events. Then she explains that she would love for the whole board to know as much about their program as the executive board does.

She goes on to ask them to consider a board member orientation at the beginning of each board term that involves spending a day at the center with the director and touring all the classrooms. The executive committee agrees to discuss this possibility and get back with her about their decision.

In the meantime, Melissa begins inviting each board member to all of their center-wide events like the fall festival, the annual art show, and the spring music program. She also includes the board members in the weekly newsletter emails and invites them to volunteer on parent workdays and to be guest readers in the classrooms. Finally, she makes an effort to send each board member a handwritten thank-you card for every time they come to the center to give their time.

DISCUSSION QUESTIONS

- Do you believe that Melissa was a good advocate for her childcare program? Did she do enough?
- What are some other ways that she could have involved the board members to show them what the center was doing to benefit families?

Chapter 15

A Sticky Situation with Facility Management

Malcolm's childcare program is only five years old. When the program opened five years ago, the building was brand-new and specifically designed to be a childcare facility. During the first year that the building was open, it was under warranty with the general contractor who designed and created the facility. Many of the facility problems during that first year had to do with a faulty part being installed, and the contractor fixed those issues immediately.

After the first year, many of the major appliances (e.g., the HVAC system, the kitchen appliances, and the generator) had extended warranties from their manufacturers, so Malcolm was able to contact the company that made each product and have them do the maintenance without any additional fees. Now that the building is five years old, all of the extended warranties have now expired.

This spring has had many thunderstorms, and one of storms has caused some significant damage to the building. Last week's storm caused a branch to fall off a tree on the backside of the property and damage a section of the roof. Also, there was a substantial power outage during the storm, and the backup generator did not come on to keep the building's essential electrical systems running. All of the center's food in the deep freezer was ruined while the power was out for a day and a half. The insurance company has come to the program site to assess the damage, but it has not determined the dollar amount needed to fix the damage or recommended any specific vendors.

Malcolm has a degree in nonprofit management that greatly assists him with running an early childhood education program, but he has never had to do facilities work himself. There is an advisory board for the childcare program that assists in decision making for the mission statement, annual budget, and community involvement activities, but the board has never had a facilities committee because the building was so new.

Malcolm called one roofing company to get a bid for the damage to the roof, but when the bid came back, it seemed too expensive for the amount of labor that it would take to repair the damage. Malcolm decided to call the manufacturer of the generator to see if there is a local repair company that it would recommend. During his phone call he found out that the extended warranty lasted for an additional two years, and the company could repair the generator with only a small co-pay from Malcolm.

As Malcolm attempted to contact contractors to repair the roof, he realized that his center does not have a contact list of preferred vendors that they can call for any type of facilities work. He would prefer to have a more streamlined system in place with a designated plumber, electrician, contractor, and handyman who already knew him and knew the facility whenever he has to make a phone call. Since the center does not have a repairman on staff, Malcolm will be responsible for completing most of the facilities work, and he would feel more comfortable working with a vendor that he knows will give him a reasonable price. Also, since the center is a nonprofit educational program, it is possible that he could find a contractor who would be willing to give the center a discount on the work.

Since the center is already five years old, it is possible that there is preventative maintenance that should be done several times a year to avoid situations like the generator giving out during an emergency. How often should Malcolm have someone come to the facility to do preventative maintenance, and is there a vendor that can regularly set up these appointments and keep the program on the schedule?

How should Malcolm proceed with all of his concerns? What steps should be taken first to resolve the situation?

REMINDERS

- Anytime you are dealing with a facilities issue, the top priority is to make sure that repairs are made quickly to sustain a healthy and safe environment for the children.

- It is always essential to get multiple estimates on facility repairs to make sure that every bid offered by a contractor is a reasonable price.
- Developing a relationship with certain vendors does not only give the center a designated contact person for contractual work, but the relationship may allow the contractor to prioritize the center's work over other jobs (especially when the contractor understands that to remain open the childcare program must meet state and federal regulations for the health and safety of young children).
- Entering an agreement with a contractor to do regular preventative maintenance on the facility may allow the contractor to offer the facility a discount on emergency repairs.
- Use resources like recommendations of the advisory board or other local center directors to find contractors who are efficient and charge a reasonable price for the work needed.

ACTION PLAN

Malcolm decides that he needs to get two more bids from contractors to repair the roof. He contacts the advisory board and local directors to see if they can offer any recommendations. He repeatedly hears the names of two different roofing companies, so he calls both of them to schedule a time for each to visit the property and see the damage to the roof. Both of these companies offer Malcolm a much lower bid than the first company, and Malcolm decides to select the roofer that is a business associate of a member of his advisory board. Mr. Griffin, the board member, suggested that he may be able to negotiate a contract for this roofer to do all of the contractual work on the center for a reduced rate.

Malcolm also sets up an appointment with the company that made the generator to come and repair it. He asks the maintenance man to bring information about how often the generator should be routinely serviced to best insurance that it functions properly. After reviewing the extended warranty that he found on the generator, Malcolm decides to make a timeline of each warranty for current appliances and facilities systems in the building. He also creates a calendar for the maintenance schedules of the systems based on the warranty information provided by the company.

After the immediate repairs are completed, Malcolm calls a board meeting to discuss putting new facility procedures into place. He asks the board for their recommendations on many different types of vendors and if the committee has a connection with any vendors that may be willing to do pro bono work or work at a reduced rate. Several of the committee members leave with a list of names that they plan to contact. Malcolm agrees to contact other vendors to see what the cost of routine maintenance would be for plumbing, electrical work, small facility repairs, and maintenance of the kitchen appliances and emptying the grease traps. If the committee did not have a personal contact, then Malcolm decided to obtain three bids for the maintenance to find the best cost. Malcolm also asked to meet with the board, or a subcommittee of the board, twice a year (before the winter and before the summer) specifically to address all facility issues.

DISCUSSION QUESTIONS

- Did Malcolm address all the essential questions?
- Would it be easier to have a facilities manager to take care of these issues? What would be the benefits and the drawbacks to relying on a facilities manager?
- Did Malcolm address enough preventative maintenance to assist the program with future facility problems?
- Who should be responsible for making future decisions on facility management, Malcolm or the committee?
- If the committee is responsible for making future facility management decisions, will Malcolm still be responsible for emergency decisions, or will he need to get approval from a committee member?

Chapter 16

A Sticky Situation with Weather Cancellations

Rosa is the owner and director at Emory's Child Development Center. Emory is a small town in the Southeast that usually only has a few bad snowstorms each winter. Because Emory is a smaller town, the city government does not always have the equipment to effectively clear the roads during winter weather, especially inside neighborhoods and in the more rural areas on the outside of town. Public schools usually close when more than an inch or two of snow is expected, but the town's private school system, the local college, most small businesses, and the hospital almost never close regardless of the amount of snow.

Many of Rosa's staff members have children enrolled in the public school system, and they may have no childcare for their children if Rosa's center remains open when public school is canceled. Even though the staff would like to cancel when the public school system is canceled, the families enrolled at the center want it to remain open despite the winter weather. Most of the parents who have children at the center work at the hospital or local small businesses, so it is an inconvenience for them to find childcare if the center closes when the public schools close.

When there is accumulated snow on the roads, it can be very difficult for all of Rosa's staff to get to work safely. Several of Rosa's teachers live in surrounding counties, and they drive more than thirty minutes to get to work. Rosa must maintain the mandatory student-to-teacher ratios in order to stay open during these snow storms, so it is concerning when staff members are prevented from traveling to the center.

On the other hand, the number of children who come to school during a snow storm is always less than normal because some families choose to keep their young children home from school if they have older children who are off from public school. The problem for Rosa is that she does not know in advance how many of the children will stay home and how many will still need childcare.

If a snow storm is predicted, Rosa usually wakes up at about 4:00 a.m. to see how much snow has accumulated and what schools and businesses have already canceled. If she has time, she tries to get into her car and drive around the neighborhood to see how slick the roads are from ice or snow. The parents always want to know as soon as possible if she is going to cancel school for the day so that they can attempt to make other childcare arrangements. She tries to make a final decision by 5:30 a.m. since the child development center opens at 6:30 a.m. This way parents are not already traveling to the center when the decision is made.

If she makes the decision to cancel, Rosa contacts the local news stations that broadcast the weather cancellations on their live news and on their websites. Rosa also uses a text message notification system to notify her staff and families that school will be canceled for the day.

Two weeks ago Rosa canceled school for a snowstorm, and by noon all of the roads in town were clear and drivable. Rosa decided to cancel because her neighborhood roads seemed very slick and because the public school system closed for the day. Since then, the parents have complained to her that she closed the center unnecessarily and they need more consistent childcare.

Rosa does not want to close every time that the public school system closes, but she must make sure that she has enough staff to keep the building open. She also wants a consistent system for families to rely on for school cancellations. How should she select when she should close her program due to winter weather? Is she doing everything possible to notify parents about weather cancellations?

REMINDERS

- The safety of the staff and the safety of the children should always be the largest consideration when deciding if a childcare program should be closed for the day.
- Childcare is a small business, as well as a school. If the facility is not open when the families need it to be open, then they will select a center that is open and meets their needs.

- It is important to remember that when a director makes a decision to stay open or close due to inclement weather, it is impossible to make everyone happy!

ACTION PLAN

Rosa decides that if the public school system cancels for the day, then her center will have an automatic one-hour delay to allow her staff more time for the roads to be cleared and to navigate their neighborhoods. Also, this helps parents with their expectations of when the center will open.

Instead of spending her time in the morning driving around her own neighborhood to assess how dangerous the roads are, Rosa decides that she will close the child development center for the full day if the local college closes. The college does not cancel classes for the day if the snow accumulation is minor, but it will cancel for significant amounts of ice and snow. Again, Rosa believes that this standard will at least give parents an idea of what to expect during winter storms. If staff members who live outside of town are not able to arrive at work due to weather conditions, they must notify Rosa as soon as possible, but at minimum one hour in advance.

Rosa decides that her current notification system with the news stations and the text message system is sufficient for notifying parents. She believes that each family must take the initiative to sign up for the text message system or to check the local news stations. Rosa is going to make sure that she sends out a reminder email and flyer to families each October about signing up for the text message system and to remind each family about the weather cancelation policy.

DISCUSSION QUESTIONS

- Do you believe that Rosa's weather cancellation policy will assist most families and still keep staff members from driving in unsafe weather conditions?
- Should Rosa make any other accommodations to notify families about a weather cancellation, or are her current methods enough?

Chapter 17

A Sticky Situation with Staff Interviews

Marlena's child development center has recently had more staff turnover than is typical. One long-term employee moved out of state with her family, and she left an assistant teacher opening in one of the preschool classrooms. Marlena also has an opening for a lead teacher in the two-year-olds classroom and an assistant teacher in the infant room. These two positions have been harder to fill.

Marlena has hired two different teachers to work in the two-year-olds classroom. One stayed at the center for about two weeks before she told Marlena that the job was not what she anticipated and resigned. She felt that too much was expected of the teaching staff when working with such young children. The other teacher worked for almost six weeks before Marlena terminated her position during the probation period. This teacher was having a hard time understanding how to use positive redirection as a tool in the classroom and seemed too harsh to work with toddlers. After several rounds of interviews, Marlena must begin looking for qualified teachers again.

Before beginning the next round of interviews, Marlena sat down to review her notes from the previous interview candidates. Every candidate she hired this year has performed well during the interview, and Marlena thought that the candidates would do well in the positions she offered them. It seems like the interview process needs to be reevaluated.

Currently, Marlena submits an advertisement to a local employment website and accepts applications for a two-week window. Once she has all the applications, she sits down to review the applications to look for previous experience in childcare, education or training in the field of early childhood education, and the applicant's length of employment at past jobs. She prefers to select candidates who have previous experience and have worked in their current job for at least a year. Marlena typically selects three or four candidates to interview, based on how many people apply for the job.

During the interview, Marlena looks to see if the candidate arrives on time and if he or she is professionally dressed. She usually asks a few questions about why the candidate wants to work in the field of early childhood education and then reviews the job description for the position. Before the candidate leaves, she takes him or her on a tour of her program to see what the classrooms look like and how the teachers interact with the children. Marlena asks each candidate to provide references, but she does not consistently do reference checks. She may contact the reference if she already knows that person and can trust his or her honest opinion. So many employers will only tell you if the candidate is eligible for rehire, and Marlena doesn't feel like that information is helpful.

After the last round of interviews, Marlena noticed that the assistant teacher and lead teacher job descriptions are not completely up-to-date. They do not include information about the center's assessment tool or how frequently the teaching staff needs to assess the children during the school year. Marlena also needs to add information about parent-teacher conferences and school-wide events like the annual fall festival that may take place after the center's normal business hours. After reviewing the job descriptions, Marlena decided to review the employee handbook also. She realized that the job descriptions, as well as teacher professionalism expectations, needed to be updated to give potential staff members an accurate idea of the job responsibilities.

Finally, Marlena decided to ask her staff and some of her colleagues who are program directors what they would look for in an interview. Several staff members suggested that Marlena include a coworker in the interviews, particularly a teacher from the classroom with the open position. A newer staff member felt like the interview process was fine, but she suggested that the interview did not fully prepare her for her new position. She thought Marlena needed to offer a new staff orientation before sending new staff members into the classroom.

A colleague at another childcare program suggested that Marlena conduct two-part interviews with a typical interview for the first step and a working interview for the second step. The other program director said that she conducts three-hour working interviews for all candidates who are finalists for a position. The candidate would have to fill out the same forms as a volunteer in order to be in the room with children. Then the candidate would participate in the classroom under the direction of the lead teacher. The candidate gets a better idea of what the job will be like, and the lead teacher can assess the candidate and report back to the director. Her colleague said that she typically uses the same classroom for infant-toddler working interviews and the same classroom for preschool working interviews because she has veteran staff in the interview who can accurately assess the candidate's ability to work with the children.

Another director explained to Marlena that she never does an interview by herself. It is always better to have at least two people to offer their perspective on the candidate. She also told Marlena that she never hires anyone without checking with three references, even if the employer tells her that the candidate is not eligible for rehire, which still tells her that person had some type of difficulty completing their job responsibilities. Also, the director told Marlena that she requires a medical release for all potential candidates stating that he or she is physically capable of meeting the job expectations.

Both directors stated that all new employees have a probation period at the beginning of their employment, and one director explained that the first day of employment consists of new employee orientation and helping the new employee set up a professional growth plan that includes all the training he or she will need to obtain in the first year of employment.

After reviewing her current hiring process and listening to suggestions from colleagues, it is obvious that Marlena needs to update the interview process for new staff.

REMINDERS

- The job description and employee handbook give an employee his or her first impression of the job expectations. The employer must express those job expectations accurately.
- A potential candidate for employment is trying to impress the employer during the interview process. If he or she does not

exhibit professionalism during the interview process, it is highly unlikely that he or she will exhibit professionalism after the interview process.
- A working interview gives the employer the opportunity to see how the candidate interacts with young children for more than just a few minutes. It also gives the candidate a very concrete way of seeing the job expectations before being hired.
- An employer can easily hire a qualified candidate for a teaching position, but that candidate must be trained in order to meet the expectations of the position. The employer cannot assign blame to an employee who had not been trained to complete his or her job.

ACTION PLAN

Marlena decides to begin by updating the current job descriptions for each position in the center. For the teaching staff, she includes conducting regular developmental assessments on the children, leading two parent-teacher conferences each school year, and participating in school-wide family events in the job descriptions. Since many of the employment websites no longer charge by the word, she decides that she will post the entire job description on the websites when looking for new employees.

Marlena also updates the employee handbook. In the section on staff professionalism, she includes expectations that employees will arrive in time to be in the classroom when they are scheduled to work, will wear professional clothing that meets the program dress code, and will follow the school's confidentiality policy, including social media and technology guidelines.

Marlena also decides that the center will switch to two-part interviews with a face-to-face interview and a working interview. The face-to-face interview will be conducted by at least two staff members, one administrator and one member of the teaching staff. During the working interview, candidates will be notified in advance to complete the required volunteer paperwork packet and to block off three hours to spend in the classroom.

Marlena is going to train two of her veteran teachers, one from a one-year-olds classroom and one from a preschool classroom, on what to look for during a working interview. She will create an evaluation form that they can use after the working interview to assess the candidate's performance and turn back in to the administration. She also decides to check at least two references for each candidate recommended for hire and to document those reference checks in the new employee's personnel folder.

After the interview is complete, Marlena is going to schedule each new employee to spend the first day of work as new employee orientation. This will include completing paperwork for human resources (payroll, insurance, etc.), but it also will include an administrator guiding the new employee through the employee handbook and assisting the employee with a professional development plan. The employee will remain on probation for ninety days, and a mentor teacher will be assigned during that time period to answer additional questions for the employee. If the new employee is an assistant teacher, then the mentor teacher may be the lead teacher for their classroom; however, if the new employee is a lead teacher, then the mentor teacher may be a lead teacher in a different classroom.

DISCUSSION QUESTIONS

- Do you believe that Marlena's changes will improve the interview process at her center?
- How do you think that currently employed staff will respond to the new interview process?
- How will Marlena be able to tell if the new process works effectively?
- Should she set a time period to evaluate if the changes are working? How long should she try this particular process before evaluating its effectiveness?

Chapter 18

A Sticky Situation with Parent Education Nights

Oxford Early Learning Academy has just entered the accreditation process, and the director, Allison, is reviewing ways to improve parent-staff communication. In order to obtain the state accreditation level that the center is seeking, Allison must offer at least four family activities per year.

During school tours for potential families, people are always asking Allison how the school prepares children for kindergarten. Parents usually want to know if children will graduate from the Early Learning Academy reading and writing their names. Allison often struggles to explain to parents all the skills that children need to be ready for kindergarten, outside of academic skills. She decides that a structured parent education night on kindergarten readiness would not only meet a requirement of the accreditation process but also help families better understand what types of skills the staff members are teaching the children.

As Allison sits down to plan the event, she realizes that she needs to determine where the education night will be held, who the speakers will be, and the length of the program. Since Oxford Early Learning Academy is a full-day early childhood program, the families with a child enrolled all work. Allison needs to pick a time that most families would have available to attend, preferably a night or weekend.

Since most of the families are involved in evening activities, she will need to provide the date in advance so that families can attend. If the program is going to be held on a night or weekend, she may need to provide childcare for the families so that they can attend. Providing childcare will mean that Allison will need staff volunteers to stay late, and she will have to have the additional funds to pay them for their work time.

The Early Learning Center has several beautiful classrooms, but there is not one large room with open space for many different adults to attend this type of event. If some of the furniture is rearranged in the largest preschool classroom, then it may have enough space for the meeting, but the staff would need to know an estimate in advance to prepare for the families. If the largest preschool classroom is used for the parents, then Allison would also need to determine where a childcare room would be located if childcare is provided.

After Allison selects a date for the parent education night, she needs to find a successful way to get this information out to each family. The school currently uses a monthly paper newsletter, a school-wide social media page, and a text message alert system as the main methods of communication. Despite these different strategies, it always seems like some parents arrive at school the day after a family event and say that no one told them about it. The staff members need to make sure that each family knows about the event and knows in advance.

The parent education night also needs to have a featured speaker. Allison and all of her preschool teachers could easily give a presentation on kindergarten readiness, but the families may receive the information better from an outside source. If a speaker from the community comes in and gives the same information the teaching staff have already been giving the families, then the parents may begin to see the validity of the information. Allison could ask a representative from the local public school system, like a current kindergarten teacher, to come and speak. Then if parents had additional questions about kindergarten, the teacher could also offer a question-and-answer session.

If the Early Learning Academy wants to focus the presentation on more than academic skills, then Allison needs to let the speaker know that the presentation would include information on preparing the whole child (e.g., health and social and emotional skills) for kindergarten. She also needs to tell the presenter how long he or she will need to speak and how long the presenter should allow for answering questions. Finally, the presenter will need to know what type of resources the Early Learning Academy will be providing (e.g., handouts and a projector).

Allison needs to create a plan for her parent education night and begin advertising it to the families. What decisions should she make?

REMINDERS

- Even very knowledgeable families have a perception of kindergarten readiness which may be very different from that of preschool programs. Most families look at the requirements of the public school system, instead of the developmental milestones of the child. Early childhood educators have a responsibility to explain child development and early education to the families they partner with in their centers.
- All families have very busy lifestyles, especially those families with all adults working outside the home. In order to have high participation at a family event, parents must know in advance, the center must communicate with the families about the event, and there must be some type of "hook" that motivates the families to attend.
- A well-planned school event includes making arrangements in advance for the space, the speaker, the topic the speaker is covering, and possible childcare. The administrator also needs to consider the cost of the speaker and childcare during the planning process.
- Food is also an excellent way to encourage families to attend an event, but the cost of providing the meal needs to be considered in the planning process.

ACTION PLAN

Allison decides to begin by contacting one of the kindergarten teachers at a local elementary school to speak to the parents. She asks Mrs. Ramsey, the teacher, to look at her calendar for February of the current school year and check her availability. Mrs. Ramsey accepts the invitation, and she tells Allison that she is available on February 17. That gives Allison just over three months to plan.

Allison decides that she is going to make the evening a family event by offering a spaghetti dinner before the presentation from the speaker, and then after the dinner, the children can go to childcare. The spaghetti dinner will begin at 5:00 p.m. while parents are still picking up children from the center, and the parent education presentation will begin at

6:00 p.m., once the center is closed. With a current kindergarten teacher that parents can ask questions and a free meal, Allison believes that the families have enough motivation to attend.

Allison asked Mrs. Ramsey to speak about the skills that children will need to enter kindergarten and what kindergarten will be like once the children begin the school year. Mrs. Ramsey will be speaking for approximately forty-five minutes, and then there will be about fifteen minutes for parents to ask additional questions.

Allison is going to collaborate with the staff and ask them to have an individual conversation with each family in their classroom in the month leading up to the event. The center will also use the school newsletter and the social media page to advertise the event. On the day of the parent education night, the school will send out a text message reminder to each family.

Finally, Allison is going to ask for staff volunteers to stay and staff the childcare room during the meeting. Parents will be asked to sign up for childcare in advance so that the school can provide the appropriate teacher-to-child ratio for students who are staying. If staff members volunteer to stay to provide childcare, they will be eligible to win a free lunch on the following week in order to encourage more staff members to sign up. All staff members are encouraged to attend the event.

DISCUSSION QUESTIONS

- Did Allison find a good "hook" to draw families in and attend the parent education night?
- Will Allison be able to plan appropriately for the number of families who will be in attendance?
- Will the parent communication be sufficient to let every family know about the event?

Chapter 19

A Sticky Situation with Fund-Raising

The cost of childcare continues to be a huge burden for all families who have one or more children enrolled in full-time care. Olivia has managed to keep the cost of tuition at her program reasonable, but she has had to increase tuition by small increments each year. These tuition increases have primarily covered the increased costs of food, facility costs, and consumable materials for the children and families (art supplies, replacement of broken toys, and center-wide family events). It has been several years since Olivia has been able to offer her teaching staff a raise.

She knows that many centers in the area are starting to offer their staff members higher pay rates than her center. Olivia had two successful interviews in the past couple of months where she offered a qualified candidate a teaching position, but the candidate declined her offer, in order to accept a position at another center with a higher pay scale. Also, Olivia has had two staff members resign this semester to accept positions at centers that pay more. She needs to find a way to improve the program's pay scale, but the current budget does not have any extra funds for a salary increase.

Increasing the tuition rate again is not a choice. Some of the center families are already struggling to pay the current cost, and it has not been a full year since the last increase took effect. Olivia needs to find additional funding that will not affect her currently enrolled families. She decides to begin her search by contacting several of her colleagues who are also center directors and asking them how they obtain additional income for their centers.

Several of the local childcare and preschool programs are doing large-scale fund-raising events with silent auctions, a renowned keynote speaker, and a buffet dinner for their participants. These events occur only one time a year, but the directors at the centers say that they must begin planning for the events over six months in advance. These fund-raisers also have a large overhead cost for the rental of the facilities, the food, and the entertainment or the speaker.

One director told Olivia that although the center did not lose any money on their event, the cost of the event only allowed the center to make a profit of $2,000. Based on the amount of time that went into the preparation, a $2,000 profit does not sound like a good use of the center resources; however, the fund-raising night did provide many people in the community with information about the childcare program and what they offer.

One of the parents at Olivia's childcare program has mentioned that the center may be an excellent candidate to receive local grants. When Olivia goes to speak with the parent to ask more questions, she finds out that grant writing typically requires no overhead cost. One of the disadvantages of this fund-raising approach is that Olivia has no previous grant-writing experience, and many grant applications can be extremely complicated. Grants also require the recipient to collect information throughout the grant period to justify how the grant funding was spent, so receiving and spending the grant funds can easily turn into a year-round project.

Olivia decides to begin looking for possible grants for which the center can apply, but by reading several grant applications Olivia realizes that there are very few grants that allow funds to go toward general operating costs (e.g., wages and facility costs). Most of the grant applications that she reviewed were focused toward a specific project like a playground renovation. These grants could still be beneficial for the center, but they do not help her current situation.

Olivia's daughter is in a local elementary school, and their program uses more traditional methods of fund-raising. The school sells wrapping paper, tubs of cookie dough, and scented candles throughout the school year. Most of these fund-raisers require each individual family to sell items to their family members and neighbors instead of the school selling the items to the community. This approach would not create a great deal of work for Olivia, but she does not know how successful it would be.

Olivia runs a full-day childcare program, and all the families of the children work during the day. Olivia also knows that for her daughter's school fund-raiser, the parents of the children at the school ended up spending most of the money on the candles and wrapping paper, not community members. If Olivia is trying to avoid raising tuition and placing more financial burden on each family, then she doesn't want the families to provide all the money for the fund-raising either.

One of the preschool programs that Olivia contacted had a lot of success with an annual 5K race in the spring and a community block party in the fall. The block party was planned on Friday evening before the local high school football game, so many community members came to tailgate before the game. The director was able to get food vendors to donate most of the food for the block party. The 5K race was also successful.

The town in which Olivia lives has a large number of runners who participate in local races, and the center was able to get corporate sponsors for the race that covered all of the overhead costs. The program raised over $6,000 last year on the combination of the two events. The trickiest part for both events was getting the permit for the block party and reserving the space for the road race.

Finally, many of the local directors mentioned the idea of school-wide events that contained a raising component. For example, several schools had an annual art show where the children's artwork was displayed throughout the school in the evening. Families could come and attend the event to see what the children were working on in their classrooms and talk with the classroom teachers.

At the end of these evenings the schools typically auctioned off pieces of the artwork. One school used a silent auction for one piece of artwork from each child, and parents and grandparents competed to win the prize. Another school had each classroom create a piece of group artwork, and they auctioned it off at the end of the evening, allowing the different families enrolled in that classroom to compete with the highest bid. These art shows served a dual purpose since the schools' accreditation required them to have at least three family involvement activities over the course of the school year. Another school did a similar fund-raising event with a school-wide chili cook-off.

For Olivia to give each of her sixteen staff members a raise of fifty cents per hour, she would need to raise an additional $16,000 per year.

She is willing to put in additional time to begin fund-raising, but this would only be one aspect of her job, so it cannot be too time consuming.

REMINDERS

- When evaluating a successful fund-raiser, you need to think about the cost that goes into the fund-raiser as well as the final profit. Do you have the funding the first year to pay for the initial costs before you get the profit?
- Grant writing is an extremely competitive process, so there is no guarantee that you will receive funding (or the full amount of the requested funding) once you submit the grant application.
- Currently enrolled families and board members can be some of a center's greatest assets when planning fund-raising strategies, especially if the program director does not have a business background. Do not forget to use all of the resources that are available to the program, especially the people who can help.
- Sustaining a successful fund-raising program requires some continuity with the individuals involved. If you plan a large-scale event one year, will several of the people who organized the event still be around to supervise the following year (staff and volunteers)?

ACTION PLAN

Olivia begins the fund-raising process by going to her advisory board with her concerns about competitive wages and her idea to organize a fund-raising committee for the childcare program. She asks for volunteers from the advisory board, and she asks if she can open the invitation up for currently enrolled families. After board members and families have had a chance to respond to her invitation, four parents and two board members have agreed to sit on the committee, including the board treasurer.

Olivia schedules the first meeting for the committee and begins by sharing the same information from the board meeting about wages and fund-raising options so that all committee members see the same purpose for the committee. The committee decides to begin the first year with a goal of raising the wage of each staff member by fifteen cents per hour. That would require $5,000 of profit from the fund-raising committee. If the committee raises more than the required $5,000, then the additional profit will all go toward increasing staff salary.

The committee agrees that they would like to bring in community funds to support the staff raises, instead of asking families to continue to give more money to the center. They decide to begin the first year with one community event, and see how successful it is. One of the parents on the committee suggests a street carnival since the program has a very visible location and the parking lot would allow for many on-site activities. The committee decides that the street carnival will include a cash raffle, lunch or dinner, and carnival rides. They also decide to include local craft vendors that agree to pay a set cost to set up their booth on the property.

One parent offers to contact local food vendors to get donations so the center will not have any cost for the food they will sell. The board treasurer volunteers to obtain a permit to hold the raffle. The other board members will contact several local businesses to obtain a corporate sponsor for the event and provide the start-up funds.

A second parent has a colleague who does graphic design and may be willing to donate his time to design the advertising for the event. Olivia agrees to organize the parent and staff volunteers for the day before and the day of the carnival. She is also going to contact local news stations in an attempt to get them to cover the story about the carnival and get additional publicity. The final parent agrees to contact local vendors that may want to participate at the carnival and a local company from which the school can rent carnival rides. The committee will meet again in two weeks to follow-up on their progress.

DISCUSSION QUESTIONS

- Did you agree with Olivia's steps to begin fund-raising for her program?
- Out of the many fund-raising options available, did the committee select a reasonable option for a childcare program of this size?
- If the street carnival is successful at raising additional funds for teacher raises, what could be the next step for the fund-raising process?

Chapter 20

A Sticky Situation with Staff Turnover

Maria is the director of a childcare program with thirty-two staff members, including herself. Her teaching staff is paid hourly and makes between $10 to $13 per hour based on their years of experience and their degree of education. All of the full-time employees are eligible for medical health insurance and dental insurance, but because Maria runs a small business, the insurance annual deductible is high and the office visit co-pays are also high.

The plan does have low co-pays for medication, and the staff really appreciate that when they have a family member who is ill. Full-time staff members also have paid time off for illness and personal time for vacations. The part-time employees do not receive paid vacation time, but they do receive some paid time off for illness proportionate to how much they work each month. Compared to many childcare programs in the area, Maria's program takes good care of its employees.

Although Maria has a small number of employees who have been at the center over five years, it is not typical for her employees to stay at the center longer than a year. In fact, she usually starts to see staff turnover between six and twelve months. Occasionally, she will hire a staff member who does not last longer than a month or two, but that is not the norm for her employees.

Because her center has been able to maintain lower student-to-teacher classroom ratios and since the center has a well-known accreditation, she has been able to attract highly educated staff members.

The problem is that these degreed employees will leave when they are offered a higher-paying job from the public school system or the city's home visitor program. In the past three months she has lost three staff members to her competitors, and several families have told her that they are upset that their children have a new teacher during the middle of the school year.

Maria presented her advisory board with information about the staff turnover, and the board treasurer stated that there is no money for employee raises at this time. She needs to come up with more creative ways to encourage staff members to stay at her center longer.

Even though she can't offer raises, the staff members really enjoy the lower student-to-teacher ratios. Teachers who previously worked for other programs tell her that they feel more relaxed in the classroom due to the smaller number of students. Are there other incentives, like lower ratios, that she could use to encourage her teaching staff? Many centers try to recognize staff who are doing their job well or encourage staff members by allowing the parent committee to provide potlucks or other special treats. Would this work for her staff?

Eight staff members out of thirty-two have a child enrolled in the childcare program, and four staff members have their child at another childcare program because they cannot afford the center's tuition rates. Staff members pay full price for childcare, but staff members may stay at the center longer if their children were at the center with them and they were paying reduced tuition.

At least two staff members resigned in the past year due to the birth of a new baby. The cost of the tuition to enroll their babies in the program was not worth keeping their jobs at the facility. Even though the advisory board could not issue a raise for the entire staff, could they offer staff members a discounted tuition rate to encourage them to stay? What information would Maria need to provide the advisory board to consider this idea?

What are the most cost-effective ways to encourage staff members to stay on her staff? How can Maria make staff members feel more supported by her program? When parents ask why staff members are leaving, what can Maria tell them about how she supports the staff? How do you explain the higher rates of turnover in the field of early childhood education?

REMINDERS

- Since early childhood education programs are not government-subsidized like public schools, the tuition collected from families is almost the total income to pay the staff, pay for the facility, and purchase resources like meals and art supplies. Increasing staff salary almost always has a direct impact on the tuition collected from enrolled families.
- Providing benefits like health insurance and paid time off is one of the best ways to reduce staff turnover.
- Teachers who feel appreciated and have a pleasant work environment are more likely to stay in their teaching positions, even if they could make a slightly larger salary at another childcare program.

ACTION PLAN

Maria decides to begin by going to the health insurance broker and asking the company to find the best health insurance package for her staff, even if that means selecting another health insurance company. Since health insurance is so important to many of her staff members, Maria wants to make sure that their insurance package can provide the best possible care at the lowest cost. The broker begins to look for better offers, and they are able to select a new company that will even allow her small business to offer a lower-cost option with fewer benefits as well as a higher-cost plan with more coverage and lower deductibles.

Since the advisory board cannot issue a staff raise, Maria decides to create a proposal for discounted child tuition for staff members. Maria creates a proposal for both a 25 percent discount and 50 percent discount for the current staff members who have young children. She also contacts several local childcare programs and asks what type of tuition discounts that those programs offer to their staff members.

Most programs explain that they offer a 50 percent discount for teaching staff, and they confirm that many of their teachers stay for several years while their young children complete their early childhood education. Although this is not a discount that each staff member will utilize, it is a staff benefit that will raise staff morale.

While the board considers this option, they encourage Maria to begin by implementing more staff appreciation activities like an employee of the month, a staff appreciation board with postings from families, and incentives for staff members who do not call in sick. Maria announces that any staff member who does not call in sick during the course of the school year will earn an additional paid vacation day at the end of the program year.

Finally, Maria decides to contact the parents at the early childhood program to create a teacher appreciation committee. Maria helps the parents organize a group that can plan appreciation events throughout the year, like a teacher appreciation week. The families decide to contact community agencies and ask for donations instead of asking the same families who are enrolled to provide additional money. The families begin by planning a staff appreciation luncheon in October just to say thank you to the staff for their hard work.

DISCUSSION QUESTIONS

- Even though Maria and her advisory board cannot provide raises to all the staff members, do you think the changes that they made will reduce staff turnover and increase staff morale?
- Would you have taken a different approach to encourage staff members to stay at the facility longer?
- Do you think that Maria's program will be able to maintain the suggested changes?

Chapter 21

A Sticky Situation with Staff Professional Development

Every teacher in the Hillsboro Child Development Program is required to obtain eighteen hours of professional development per year. The center has a training budget to pay for teacher training, and teachers are paid for the hours that they spend in training. Katrina, the center director, has been letting staff sign up for their own training hours, and she has only been monitoring if the full eighteen hours are complete by the end of each year in order to meet the state requirements for the childcare program. A few weeks ago Katrina sat down to review staff training hours, and she found that teachers are not necessarily taking trainings that benefit their development in the classroom.

When Katrina pulled the training file of one of her infant room teachers she saw that most of Alyssa's training hours this year were focused on the preschool classroom. She took the exact same five classes that one of her friends in the preschool classroom took even though they did not benefit her current classroom setting.

Another infant room teacher, Connie, waited to start her training hours until one month before she needed to complete her training. She had to sign up for every class that she could attend after work at the local childcare resource center, including trainings on school-age child care and home-based childcare.

Katrina noticed that one of the preschool teachers took the same two-hour training four times during the past school year. Other preschool teachers have approached Katrina about how much they would like to take trainings about dealing with challenging behaviors in the classroom or working with children with special needs. When they have tried to sign up for these types of trainings in the area, they are either during the day when the teachers need to be in the classroom or they fill up too quickly.

Katrina would like to implement a new classroom curriculum next year, but she is worried about all of the staff members receiving training before the new school year begins. She wants the entire team trained on the new curriculum, not only the lead teachers. One of the local training agencies offers trainings on the curriculum a few times per month, but it will be very difficult for all thirty-two members of Katrina's staff to attend the training in the next two months. Many of the staff have evening and weekend commitments, and one training will not accommodate the entire staff.

What is the best method for Katrina to help all of her staff members meet their training hour requirement and still make sure that all of the training is pertinent to each staff member?

REMINDERS

- Teachers need to set an example for lifelong learning. It is the teacher's job to instill a love for learning in the children they care for each day. As professionals, teachers need to make an effort always to continue learning about their chosen field.
- It is the job of the staff member to make sure that he or she is taking training that will assist him or her in the classroom. Training hours should specifically relate to the job and the age group with which the teacher is working.
- It can be beneficial for coworkers to attend the same trainings so that they can implement new teaching strategies in the classroom together and hold each other accountable for the skills they have learned about in training.
- It can be very challenging for teachers to focus during evening trainings after working a full day in the classroom. Weekend trainings can be challenging for teachers also because they have worked a full week already and are now giving up their free time. The most effective training time is usually during typical work hours.

ACTION PLAN

Katrina decides that in order to make sure that her entire staff receive training on the new curriculum before the upcoming school year, she will need to schedule a training at the Child Development Program for all of the staff members. Since this will be an all-day training and an essential training for all staff, Katrina wants to schedule the training during the workweek and plan an in-service day for the teachers. She believes that if all the teachers are trained together, they will be a resource for one another as they learn the new curriculum. A whole-staff training will also give the staff an opportunity to spend time together and work on team building.

The entire staff training will total seven hours for every staff member, but each teacher will still need to attend additional eleven hours of training over the course of the year. Katrina decides that the remainder of the training hours should be linked to the staff members' professional development plan goals for the year and will be reviewed during each staff member's annual evaluation. She explains this information at the monthly staff meeting, and she also tells the teachers that anyone pursuing a degree in early childhood education and taking early education classes can still count those courses toward their professional training hours.

DISCUSSION QUESTIONS

- Would it be more effective for Katrina to schedule all of the staff annual training hours, or is it still important for staff members to select their own training as well?
- Is Katrina helping each staff member get the training that he or she needs with her new plan for professional development?
- If Katrina schedules only one center-wide training per year, how can she help staff members to find trainings on the topics that they request like dealing with challenging behaviors?
- Should staff members only be attending local trainings? Is there a way to send even a limited group to regional or national trainings and then have them share new information with the staff as a whole when they return?

Chapter 22

A Sticky Situation with Scheduling

Robert supervises thirty-seven staff members at Our House Child Development Center. Twenty-one of those employees work full time and receive paid time off for illnesses and vacation. The sixteen part-time staff members receive paid sick time if they work twenty hours per week. The child development center is closed one week for winter break, and it is closed for eight other federal holidays. It is a year-round childcare program that does not follow the same schedule as the public school system.

One of Robert's jobs as the center director is to create the weekly schedule, but this process seems to be getting more and more complicated. In the past there has been an unwritten rule that no more than two staff members can ask off for a vacation day at a time. Robert has two reliable substitute teachers who can usually assist if he gives them notification, but the center also has to plan for staff members calling in sick.

Although the center does not follow the public school system, many of the employees have children who are enrolled in public school. There is always a competition to be one of the two staff members who get approved to be on vacation during public school spring break, and those who cannot go on vacation that week are very disappointed.

Any staff member who wants to ask off for vacation, a personal day, or a scheduled doctor's appointment must ask off at least two weeks in advance so that Robert can plan the schedule accordingly. When staff members (or their family members) are sick, staff may call in the evening before their shift or in the morning before their shifts begin. If there are several staff members out sick and the substitutes are already scheduled to work, then the administration team will work in the classrooms, but this isn't ideal since Robert, his assistant director, and the office manager also have other responsibilities.

In July, Robert approved two employees for vacation for the week of public school fall break. When he posted the October schedule, there were two employees who were very upset to see their names on the schedule. One of the teachers said that she sent him an email at the beginning of the summer asking for the days off. She assumed that he approved it since he never told her that she could not have those days off. Robert has no record of this email. The other teacher was previously notified that she could not take the week off since two other employees were approved for vacation time, but when the schedule was posted, the teacher said that she knows that she asked off before the other teachers.

Robert is also struggling with how the teachers ask off for sick time. Many of the teachers have young children, so he understands that if their children are sick they need to care for them. Even though other teachers may not have young children, they work with young children every day and can be exposed to many illnesses that way. This is the reason that the center has paid sick leave. However, Robert does not like the current process for calling in sick.

Teachers who cannot attend work due to illness will either text or call Robert to notify him that they need to stay home. Sometimes Robert gets phone calls or texts in the middle of the night. He is still stunned that some staff members feel the need to leave him a message in the middle of the night, possibly waking him up in the process. Sometimes staff members call in sick minutes before their shifts are supposed to begin.

Last week Robert received a phone call from a teacher who said she was unable to come to work because she had not slept well the night before. Robert explained that since she did not have a contagious illness and since she had not asked off work in advance, she was expected to be at work. As a supervisor, Robert is a little skeptical of staff members only sending a text to say that they are ill.

The two substitutes who work for Robert's program are very reliable. They show up for work when Robert has assigned them a shift, and they know the children and families. They almost work every day to cover the two staff members who can take a vacation day, but then there is not additional staff to cover teachers who call in sick. Robert could really use more substitutes, but it is hard to find staff members who do not need to work every day. Also, substitute teachers must maintain the same background checks, training hours, and certifications that permanent staff members have. Most of the teachers with those credentials in Robert's town already have permanent positions.

Robert needs to streamline the staffing procedure at his center and find a way to make scheduling simple and to make sure that staff members know quickly if they are approved for time off. He also needs to find a way to make sure that he has adequate staff coverage at his center each day. What steps does he need to take?

REMINDERS

- Staff members who receive paid time off are more likely to stay in their positions longer than staff members who do not receive paid time off. Having lower staff turnover is beneficial to the children and appealing to the parents.
- Having a set policy on approved time off can eliminate many disputes between staff members about the center schedule.
- Using a center-wide floating teacher can eliminate the need for additional substitutes and attract teachers with higher qualifications since the floater could obtain full-time benefits.

ACTION PLAN

Robert decides that the unwritten rules for asking off of work need to be written down for all staff members to see.

1. Vacation days will be approved on a first-come, first-served basis. Only two staff members may use a vacation day on the same business day. Staff members must complete the leave request form and submit to management. The date of submission will be considered the date of the request.
2. Staff members may call in sick if they are sick or a member of their immediate family is sick. If the staff member (or the family member) is sick more than two consecutive days, then a doctor's note is

required. If the staff members have used all of the allotted sick time and continue to need additional sick time, then a doctor's note may be requested.
3. If a staff member needs to call in sick, then he or she must contact the director by phone before 10:00 p.m. or after 6:00 a.m. The staff member must contact the administration at least one hour before the staff member is expected to be at work.
4. If a staff member has not been approved for vacation time and then calls in sick on the day requested off, then the staff member will be required to provide documentation of the illness or emergency.
5. Staff members are expected to use professionalism when asking for paid time off. They must make every effort to be at work if they have not asked off in advance.
6. Vacation time will not be approved during the first three weeks of the new school year in order to provide consistency and acclimate children to their new classrooms.

Robert also decides that he needs to increase staffing just slightly to make sure that there is adequate classroom coverage even when teachers call in sick. He decides to add one full-time staff floater position. This person would work forty hours per week and receive full-time benefits, but his or her scheduled hours would change each week based on the needs of the center. Robert hopes that this will assist him with finding additional help that meets the staff requirements.

First, since they have both been excellent employees, he opens the floater position up to the two substitute teachers. One of the substitutes instantly declines because she enjoys the flexibility of her schedule. The other substitute teacher accepts the position, and Robert posts a job opening for a substitute teacher. He mentions in the job description that the position includes consistent work.

DISCUSSION QUESTIONS

- Do Robert's new policies on how to use paid leave seem reasonable for the center employees?
- Do the policies limit the employees from asking off when they need to be away from work?

- Robert had several concerns over the professionalism of staff calling in sick for work. Could he have addressed that issue more effectively?
- How will a center-wide floater benefit the program? Could it be too expensive?
- What does Robert need to look for when hiring a new substitute teacher?

Chapter 23

A Sticky Situation with Transportation

There are eighty-four children enrolled at Sunnyside Childcare Center starting in the infant room through the pre-kindergarten classroom. In past years the center had an afterschool program for elementary school students, but enrollment began to drop three years ago in the afterschool program, and it was discontinued. The center still possesses two fifteen-passenger vans that were previously used to pick up students from the elementary schools. Now the vans only get used a couple of times a year when the pre-kindergarten students go on an occasional field trip.

The state childcare licensing requirements for transportation include that any vehicle used by the childcare must have a minimum of one annual visit to the mechanic for maintenance. The last visit to the mechanic was extremely expensive. The monthly insurance premiums are becoming more expensive due to the age of the vehicle and general inflation.

The childcare regulations also require that all children transported on the vehicles must have up-to-date car seats or booster seats based on the state requirements. Although the new law has not yet gone into effect, in just two months the booster seat laws are changing, and all children under eighty pounds and under four feet, eight inches tall must sit in a booster seat. This will require every child at the center to ride in a car seat or booster seat for field trips, and the center owns only a limited amount of seats.

During the past school year, Amanda, the center director, took the pre-kindergarten class and the preschool class on two field trips. In the fall, the center took the children to the local orchard to pick apples and pumpkins, and in the spring, the center took the children to see a play at the local children's theater. Many of the parents were unable to attend the field trips, so both vans were full of students that the center had to transport to the field trips. At the end of the year program, most of the students stated that the orchard and the children's theater were two of their favorite events of the year.

Last week the owner of Sunnyside Childcare Center received the quarterly insurance bill for the vans, and she asked to meet with Amanda. Now that the center does not have an afterschool program, the vans get little use. The owner has asked Amanda to create a list of all the costs associated with the vans and bring it to their meetings.

Along with the cost of maintenance and the insurance, Amanda must also pay for each staff member who works at Sunnyside to have a background check from the Department of Motor Vehicles and keep that on file for childcare licensing. Those staff members who are approved to drive the van must submit to random drug testing throughout the year. All of these expenses add up over the course of the year.

Is the cost of the upkeep for the two vans worth the benefit of taking the children on a few field trips each year? If the owner decides to sell the vans, how will the school offer the families an opportunity for field trips? If the school cannot offer any type of field trips, then how will the families respond?

REMINDERS

- Although a childcare center is an educational institution, it is also a small business. In any business, it is essential to look at the cost-benefit analysis of every practice. If the cost outweighs the benefit, then it can be detrimental to the business to continue that practice.
- When making a policy change in any childcare center (like discontinuing field trips), it is essential to look at the childcare licensing requirements to see what policies the center is required to follow.
- If it is not possible to continue taking the children on field trips, then how can the childcare program find an equivalent educational opportunity to supplement the curriculum?

ACTION PLAN

After meeting with the owner of Sunnyside Childcare, it is obvious to Amanda that it is too expensive to continue to pay for the vans when they are used so sparingly. The owner decides that she is going to sell the vans and cancel the insurance policy; however, the childcare license for Sunnyside Childcare Center currently states that the center provides transportation.

Before the insurance policy can be canceled, Amanda must contact childcare licensing and alter the center's license and remove transportation. Sunnyside must receive a copy of the new childcare license with the transportation component removed before the vans can be sold and insurance policy can be canceled. If not, the childcare program could be cited for a licensing violation.

During the meeting, Amanda and the center owner discuss different ways that Sunnyside could still provide field trips for the children enrolled. One possibility was renting transportation just for the day. Amanda, again, contacted the childcare licensing office to see if this alternative would be a possibility. The childcare licensing office said it is possible for the center to rent transportation, but Sunnyside would still be responsible for all the same requirements as if it owned the vehicle.

At the time of the annual licensing visit, the center would need to provide the name of the organization that owned the vehicle, proof of insurance and maintenance, and contact information for the company. The licensing office may have to contact the company to review the background checks of the drivers. The childcare program would also have to make sure that each child still had the proper car seat or booster seat. Amanda decided to look for other alternatives.

Although staff members would not be able to drive Sunnyside children in their own cars, it is possible for the parents to do all the transportation for their own children with no liability to the center. There was not a lot of family participation in this year's field trips, but those dates were provided to the families only about two weeks in advance. If the parents received the date of the field trip earlier, perhaps more families would be able to attend. Amanda also found out that many of the popular sites in town for field trips (e.g., the children's museum and the children's theater) offer portable field trips where the organization brings a field trip on-site to local schools.

After reviewing the information with the owner, Amanda decides that each year during one day in October, the Sunnyside Childcare Center will cancel preschool and pre-kindergarten classes and meet at the local orchard. This date will be announced at family orientation in August so that families can plan accordingly. Also, the center will negotiate a contract with the children's theater to bring two portable field trips to the center each spring. Once Amanda and the owner alter the childcare license for the center and work out the details with the children's theater, Amanda sends a letter out to the currently enrolled families to explain the upcoming changes for the center's transportation and field trips.

DISCUSSION QUESTIONS

- Did the cost of keeping the vans outweigh the benefits of taking the children on a few trips per year?
- What benefits will the center see from discontinuing transportation?
- Did Amanda do what was necessary to follow the childcare licensing laws for her state?
- How do you think families will react to the new field trip schedule for the upcoming school year?

Chapter 24

A Sticky Situation with Staff Wages

Springfield Childcare Center has been known for paying its teachers well. During the past ten years, Fatima, the director, has tried to pay her staff about a dollar more per hour than most of the centers in Springfield. This has actually been a beneficial business practice because her staff members do not turn over as quickly and therefore the families enrolled in the program tend to stay longer.

The city council has just voted to raise minimum wage by $3 an hour over the next five years. There will be three different increases to move toward the final increase of $3, so this will not happen all at one time. This increase will significantly impact the center's budget and its ability to pay a competitive salary. Most of the childcare centers in the area need to increase tuition each time the minimum wage increases.

Fatima has been slightly increasing tuition once a year at approximately a 2 percent increase to maintain cost of living adjustments and to make sure the staff members receive a small raise in compensation. The parents seem to anticipate that small increase now, but these increases will have to be larger.

Although Fatima has been at the childcare center only for ten years, she has staff members who have been with the program for up to sixteen years. Right now the compensation is not equivalent for all employees. Teachers were hired at competitive salaries at the time of hire, and since then they have been eligible for incremental salary increases.

When Fatima sat down to look at the salary rates for the budget revision, she realizes that some senior members of the teaching team are making less than employees hired four or five years later based on the competitive rate that was acceptable at that time. Fatima needs to find a way to correct that problem when creating the new pay scale.

Fatima also notices that some of the more educated teachers are being paid the same as teachers with fewer qualifications. Is there a way to set up the new salary system so that salary level depends on education and years of experience? Once the new salary scale is set, then the center will know what the tuition cost rate will be for the following year. How can Fatima best present that information to the parents?

REMINDERS

- The field of early childhood education is evolving and asking teachers to be more and more qualified for their positions. It is wonderful that more skilled teachers are working in the field of early education, but small businesses also must find realistic ways to compensate those teachers.
- The largest single cost for all childcare centers is staffing. If you think about each business selling a product, childcare centers are selling the quality of their teaching staff. In order to have a desirable product, centers must have qualified teaching staff.
- Although a professional work environment should not encourage employees to share their pay rate to compare salaries, it is still essential to find the most "fair" method of compensating its employees.
- Since professionals in the field of early childhood education are paid so little, it is not uncommon for teachers to leave one program to receive a $0.25 raise per hour at another program. A center that can maintain a higher pay scale will easily reduce staff turnover.

ACTION PLAN

Fatima's main goal while creating the new pay scale is to find a way to compensate teachers based on their education and experience to have a consistent pay scale in place. A consistent pay scale based on education and experience would prevent potential employees from bargaining with her during the interview process and prevent petty arguments between current staff members on who should be paid more.

Fatima would like a sliding scale where she can look at the candidate's education (high school diploma, CDA, early childhood associate's degree, early childhood bachelor's degree, or a master's degree in education) and then look at the years of experience at her center to select the current year's pay rate. This type of grid would be easy to use and could be public information to the staff if they were considering the benefits of increasing their education level.

Because of the gradual increase to minimal wage, Fatima will have to create three different grids to be used over the course of the next five years. To create each grid, she decides to start at fifty cents about the minimum wage for a new employee with a high school diploma. Then hourly salary will increase by degree and by years of experience.

Fatima uses the grid for the first minimum wage increase to estimate the annual staffing budget based on her current staff education and years of experience. She also estimates that the cost of food will increase due to the increase in minimum wage. She inserts those two numbers into her current budget to get a rough estimate for the total expenses for next year. If Fatima's center keeps its current enrollment, then there would be a need for a 10 percent tuition increase next year. The second and third increases are not as large as the first increase, so the following tuition increases would not be as substantial.

Since the tuition increase is so much larger than previous years, she believes that she should hold a parent meeting after the center is closed to explain the cost of the tuition increase. She contacts her administrative board to ask for support, and both the current board president and the treasurer agree to be present to answer questions. During the meeting she wants to show parents several key points directly related to the tuition increase:

- How much of the center budget is dedicated to staffing
- The sources of income that the center receives
- The educational requirements of the teaching staff based on the center accreditation

Fatima also wants to discuss the average length of employment of her teachers compared to many other childcare programs in the area. She believes that based on the general knowledge of the minimum wage increase and the parent relationships with the staff most families will accept the new tuition information. Even still, there may be a few families who look for other childcare centers based on the tuition increase.

DISCUSSION QUESTIONS

- What did Fatima do in this situation to take care of the staff members?
- What did she do to take care of the families and provide the best quality care for the children enrolled?
- Is her proposed salary scale and budget reasonable?
- Did Fatima select the best method of communication to inform the parents about the tuition increase?

About the Author

Sarah Taylor Vanover has been working in the field of early childhood for over seventeen years. She first began as an assistant teacher in an infant classroom, and since then she has served as a lead teacher, a program administrator, a trainer, and a classroom teaching coach. Dr. Vanover has also had the opportunity to work at the state-level to assist with policy development and supervise early childhood trainers throughout the Commonwealth of Kentucky.

Currently, Dr. Vanover teaches early childhood education courses and supervises student teachers at Eastern Kentucky University in Richmond, Kentucky. She completed her doctoral work in Education Policy and Leadership and focused her research on what families look for when selecting childcare for their children. She is an active trainer in Kentucky and surrounding states and frequently speaks at conferences on topics like quality childcare indicators, language development in the early childhood classroom, and the importance of assessment in early childhood education.

Dr. Vanover lives in Lexington, Kentucky, with her husband, Rob, and their two sons, Jack and James.

www.ingramcontent.com/pod-product-compliance
Lightning Source LLC
Chambersburg PA
CBHW021800230426
43669CB00006B/147